ADVANCE PRAISE FOR
HOLISTIC MARKETING

"Fantastic insight from the trenches of digital marketing transformation. This book goes beyond the theoretical to illuminate how you can create a high-performing digital marketing team."

—MARK MITTON, president, 9th Wonder Sprint

"Insightful, timely, and relevant playbook for the modern marketing challenges. This is a book that should sit on every marketing executive's desk for daily reference."

—DAVID TURNER, CEO, Velocity Now

"Definitely a book written for and by a marketer. Hits the important aspects of digital marketing transformation. Anyone that's building a team or looking at making their team more efficient should read this."

—ANA-MARIA BANTA, director of global marketing, Quantive

Digital Transformation through
PEOPLE, PROCESSES, and TECHNOLOGY

Holistic Marketing

ED LOCHER

RIVER GROVE
BOOKS

Published by River Grove Books
Austin, TX
www.rivergrovebooks.com

Distributed by River Grove Books

Design and composition by Greenleaf Book Group and Mimi Bark
Cover design by Greenleaf Book Group and Mimi Bark
Cover images used under license from ©Shutterstock.com/INAMEL

Publisher's Cataloging-in-Publication data is available.

Print ISBN: 978-1-63299-722-7

eBook ISBN: 978-1-63299-723-4

First Edition

CONTENTS

INTRODUCTION

Here's a fun game. The next time you're at a dinner party, ask a couple of people if their favorite inventory management philosophy is FIFO or LIFO. If that elicits nothing but blank stares, ask them whether they prefer GAAP to non-GAAP financial reporting. Still nothing? Then try this. Ask them for their favorite commercial. BINGO! You're going to get a response, and whether you think they're crazy or not, I'm 100% certain that they will have an opinion they can share.

Marketing, unlike so many other parts of the business world, is truly accessible to every single person. We're up to our gills in it whether we want to be or not. Digital marketing experts suggest that every individual is exposed to over 4,000 marketing messages every single day.[1] It's relentless, so much so that your brain is constantly filtering out nearly all of it. But the messages that do break through, the ones that we remember, help to convince all of us that we are experts in the ways of marketing.

People remember the specific ads that break through this tsunami of messaging because they resonate with them on a personal

---

1   Paul Jankowski, "5 Ways to Break through the Noise," *Forbes* (August 24, 2016).

level. The marketer was able to make a connection, and, to the recipient, the brain translates this into "good" marketing. This empowers people to believe they know what good marketing is.

To be sure, in order to achieve success in marketing, we must appeal to individuals. And it's no surprise then that many individuals feel they are experts. The law of probabilities suggests that some marketing, at some point, has struck a chord with them, and therefore, they have cracked the code on good marketing. But what do all individuals have in common? Not a thing. And that's precisely why marketing is different from all the other disciplines. It's subjective in ways that finance, accounting, legal, and even sales are not.

Marketing is different. Everything from the dialogue in a commercial to the color of the buttons on a landing page begins with someone's opinion of what might work. Many of these things can be tested, even in real time, but the first iteration always begins as a guess. By its nature, it is subjective and prone to personal bias. A lot of people like dogs, and if the CMO feels a dog could help move the needle, you might see a dog in the commercial. However, there is no law that states a dog must be in a truck commercial. Fines will not be imposed, and people won't be fired. This personal bias, this subjectivity, leads people to believe that they know enough about marketing to be an expert.

The fact that it doesn't work this way is overlooked by many. In fact, in my career, I have only worked for a few companies where the C-suite really understood the subjectivity and nuance of marketing. These few knew they weren't an expert and actively sought out expertise from others to help fill that void in the leadership spectrum. That doesn't mean an opinion, but they knew that it was just that—one person's opinion.

As a marketer with over two decades of experience, I can say with certainty that B2B marketing has a level of complexity that exceeds what is seen on the surface. Bringing a dog into your commercial will not increase your sales. Effective marketing is a beautiful combination of science, art, and intuition. It is subtle in ways that defy easy explanation, and these subtleties are often the difference between success and failure. It is a discipline that requires courage, fortitude, determination, and patience. Marketing as a discipline is all these things and more.

The good news is that the technology is there for marketers to address that complexity and build transparent, accountable, predictable, and scalable systems. Digital tools are absolutely instrumental to this new, more advanced state of marketing. But they are not the only piece, and that's why companies haven't realized the true value of their own investments.

Part of the problem is semantics. By focusing on the technology aspect, organizations run the risk of asymmetric investments that lead to inefficiencies and ultimately into unrealized potential. The technology is a necessary but not sufficient component if the end goal is true transformation.

So, here's the bad news. Well, maybe not bad, but challenging for sure. Digital transformation is much more than just technology. The painful truth is that it takes more than just writing a check and installing some software to create an agile and productive money-making machine that eliminates subjectivity from the equation—a whole heck of a lot more.

This brings me to the purpose of this book. Within these pages, you will discover how marketing leaders can harness the power of digital transformation to deliver predictable top-line revenue growth by eliminating subjectivity. By holistically managing the people, processes, and technology, you can create a high-performance demand generation engine. This digital transformation represents a new era in marketing, a more evolved state where data-driven decision-making supplants hunches and guesses as the engine of growth. It will fundamentally change your understanding of marketing's ability to contribute to organizational value.

The B2B marketing leaders that can lead this transition will create a sustainable competitive advantage for their organizations that leads to improved financial performance and increased valuations. The rewards also filter down to the personal level, from improving the individual's brand and marketability to increased compensation and equity. The guidelines laid out in this book can be the fuel for career acceleration and becoming a prominent leader in this new era of marketing.

THE DARK AGES OF MARKETING

Speaking of this new era, it's still early days. We've evolved more in the past 5 years than we have in the previous 15, and the pace of change is accelerating, but we're still at the beginning of the curve. What can you do to ensure your organization stays at the front?

To fully understand what's happening, we need to go back to the 1960s and 1970s, when computers and automation enabled a more disciplined and profitable approach to operations and resource use. It was birthed in the manufacturing sector and was loosely referred to as *materials* or *resource planning*. The ultimate goal of this activity was to improve the efficiency of production through better scheduling and process improvements. At the risk of oversimplification, at its core, it was an improved method that removed uncertainty and subjectivity from the process of building things by increasing visibility and removing waste.

Those companies that adopted these principles tended to

operate more efficiently and had a significant advantage over those that didn't. Natural selection at the corporate level accelerated its adoption. Over the ensuing decades, as organizations continually strived to become more efficient, this process expanded across two dimensions.

First, businesses began to apply resource planning methods to more lines of business. Engineering, project management, and financial planning and analysis all became inputs to the machine. With each addition, companies were able to extract new efficiencies. And by looking at the organization as a whole, rather than as a collection of departments where each was focused on their own set of activities, they were able to grow and scale profitability.

The second dimension came as more lines of business adopted similar principles; moving beyond inputs for manufacturing, they became sources of efficiency improvement of their own. Supply chain management embraced this philosophy, improving internal processes to increase the return on those investments. CRM, or customer relationship management, essentially did the same thing for the selling process. In both cases, the goal was to formalize, document, and automate a complex process to remove subjectivity and add scalability and visibility.

And it worked. Companies such as SAP, Oracle, Salesforce, and many other technology powerhouses have succeeded over the past couple of decades because they have powered a revolution in how business gets done.

In the boardroom, investment decisions are made based on hard data. Finance, operations, and product development all bring their perspective based on specific information as it appears in their systems, their source of truth. It's expected, even required, that these leaders come armed with the latest facts about their line of business, whether that be cash position, pipeline coverage, product release dates, or any number of other elements that factor into business decisions. They are all now based on data, not just someone's opinion. Ambiguity is anathema.

Woe be to marketing and the CMO, which have lived historically and predominantly in ambiguity. Their data, more often than not, was fuzzy. A quarter century years ago, overnights (TV ratings), direct and email responses, and impressions (for those early movers) were the best marketing could come up with. Yes, they were tangible results, but they were also nearly impossible to link to revenue with any degree of accuracy. These were a far cry from the data provided by other departments and did not provide a stable foundation when lobbying for precious company resources.

A case in point: Back at the turn of the century, the dot-com boom promised all kinds of things based on impressions, eyeballs, and clicks. It turns out that those "all kinds of things" were mostly vanity metrics that vaporized over $4 trillion (yes, that's a T) from the stock market. Ten years ago, it was likes and follows. While that sort of wealth wasn't destroyed the second time around, it was no better at predicting company success than those other metrics that came before. None of them were any better than the old overnights used before the Internet age. Measuring how many people see your message is not a good proxy for effectiveness. The inability to predict with any accuracy the result of a marketing investment was the norm. Consequently, it was still very hard to determine whether your marketing was working.

It would be hard to blame a CEO for choosing to invest in a new factory or product when presented with a robust investment case, complete with projected ROI and break-even times, when the alternative from marketing was based on a whole lot of "Trust me; this is going to be BIG!" It wasn't necessarily the CMO's fault, it's just that the tools and processes weren't available to compete on a level playing field with their peers in other areas of the business.

DAWN OF A NEW ERA

That was true of marketing in the past, but today's environment is not at all the same. Back in the day, marketing was all about campaigns. They were big and unwieldy, required a ton of resources, were fraught with peril, and if you had a genius on hand to put in charge of the whole shebang, your chances of success went up dramatically. Absent an in-house guru, many organizations outsourced this part to an agency, which had some advantages but also came with a bunch of risks. The bottom line is that each campaign was a gamble, a big bet placed on a lot of subjectivity, where the chances were higher of it being a swing and a miss than a home run. It was a complex operation where lots of things could go wrong, and the success or failure often hinged on the smallest of details.

In marketing's vernacular, it meant spending two to six months constructing a campaign. This included defining the buyer, segmenting the audience, identifying tactics, designing and producing all of the required assets, testing concepts and messages through focus groups, sourcing all of the channels, and then when all of that was ready, launching the campaign out into the wild. At that point, you may have some early indicators of the eventual success of the campaign, but the buyer response was typically delayed by weeks, if not months. This meant that you really didn't know if the campaign was effective until two to three quarters after the key decisions had been made.

Then, starting in about 2012, new tools and capabilities started to emerge that would lead to fundamental change. Technology arrived that enabled marketers to bring the same level of discipline and insight into their operations as ERP did for manufacturing or CRM did for sales. Data management systems and marketing automation platforms powered advanced segmentation and integrated outbound tactics. The Internet provided a platform for measuring response and engagement. For those companies and teams progressive enough to harness it, these new capabilities revolutionized how marketing was conducted and measured.

Using these tools allowed marketers to test and invest rather than go all in on any one particular idea. A general no longer had to commit vast amounts of resources into a fight where they had no intelligence on the enemy. The new model meant they could conduct a series of much smaller, tactical strikes, probing the enemy's defenses and using that data as a key input to the overall strategy. They didn't need to attack along a thousand-mile front. They could pick and choose their battles, allocating resources where they had the best chance of success. Don't like the looks of that reinforced embankment? Find a softer spot where you can make a breakthrough.

For marketers, this meant that, rather than developing a giant portfolio of assets around a single campaign theme, they could choose three to five ideas based on customer or prospect research, subject matter expertise, and market validation. They could then execute a limited number of tactics, creating variable combinations of messaging, subject lines, creative design, and so on, and then test these variations against their target audience, quickly assess in near real time which was performing the best, and then invest the remaining resources on the winning permutation.

This new process powers two very important improvements. First, by breaking out of the antiquated campaign process of the past, marketers are able to dramatically increase their chances of success. By building an agile process with a series of smaller investments, it is possible to invest more resources behind proven messages and tactics while simultaneously limiting the damage and waste of a failed campaign. The process itself is scalable and repeatable, bringing economies of scale to campaign execution, and it produces the same benefits that manufacturing did those many years ago.

Second, by building the infrastructure required to execute this new, agile campaign development and execution process, it is possible to extend that visibility throughout the entire pipeline, from first impression to closed-won and through contract renewal. This transforms marketing's contribution to the revenue pipeline into a simple financial conversation.

Once this infrastructure and process are in place, it's possible to quantify exactly what can be delivered and when. A sample case might look like this: A company can invest $100,000 in marketing demand generation, and, based on proven channel performance, 5.7 months later, the company can expect $1 million in closed-won revenue. There is no subjectivity here. The machine is predictable and transparent. The question now isn't "What can we get for our investment?" It's "How much revenue do we need, and how much expense will we incur?"

It is impossible to overstate the importance of this last question. Marketing now has a secure seat at the table with operations and product development and any other part of the business when lobbying for scarce company resources. It has a transparent, predictable, accountable engine with a defined ROI. Subjectivity has been removed; it's a simple question of how much expense is available to generate predictable revenue.

Not only does this change the tenor of investment decisions, but it also virtually eliminates marketing program dollar cuts.

Previously, the decision to cut from the marketing budget was an easy one because no one could quantify the impact. "Sure, you can take the money, but you're going to regret it" is not really a very compelling argument. In the system that I've just described, the conversation is very different. Of course, those dollars, euros, or yen are up for seizure, but when you can explain what the downstream impact is to revenue, all of a sudden, the conversation shifts. The predictable losses of dropping a campaign are clear. Using the previous example, if marketing is asked to return $100,000 to the business, we can and should expect a revenue impact in 5.7 months of $1,000,000 in revenue. No muss, no fuss, no ambiguity. Are you willing to take that hit to the pipeline? The answer may still be yes, but at least you know what the impact will be, and it gives marketing a fighting chance to retain their budgets.

WHAT DO YOU WANT TO BE WHEN YOU GROW UP?

Lao Tzu said, "A journey of a thousand miles starts with a single step." Yogi Berra said, "If you don't know where you are going, you'll end up someplace else." There are as many quotes as you care to find, all saying essentially the same thing: Before you start out to accomplish a goal, you need to first establish what it is that you want. You need to define success for your organization. Avoiding (or only half answering) this critical question is a common—and often catastrophic—error, so tackling that question up front before any of the downstream work is initiated is essential. What does success look like? Even if there isn't really a finish line, if you haven't at least outlined what the ultimate goal is, the chances of you achieving anything remotely close to what you set out to do are pretty slim.

With that in mind, what does today's marketing leader want to accomplish? Is it to create awareness in the market? Is it to establish credibility, or repair a tarnished image? Is it to create top-line revenue or increase the velocity of the existing pipeline?

There are lots of different goals that a marketing organization may undertake at any given moment. What makes this even more challenging is that these goals are typically not mutually exclusive. This overlap can create tension with other lines of business or within the marketing organization itself. The European sales team may want more leads, while the Americas sales team may want help converting existing opportunities. Corporate communications may want to focus on improving brand awareness, while the product team may want help creating personas and customer journey maps. There is literally no end to what a marketing organization may be called on to support. Consequently, the first and most important step in delivering value from marketing's digital transformation is defining exactly what you want to be when you grow up. What are the two or three key deliverables that marketing will commit to implementing to create value?

The best goals are those that can be described quickly, with a minimum of jargon that is easily understood by any audience. A good example would be "Marketing will increase top-line revenue growth by 20% this year and 30% in the following year." Another might be "Marketing will increase unaided awareness in our target audience by 10% this year and next." They don't necessarily have to be written like your annual review metrics. Aspiring to "Create sustainable competitive differentiation through our marketing" would be another example. The important thing is that the team—and the organization at large—can see and understand the vision of what marketing will accomplish as part of this new commitment to digital transformation. What will be different, new, easier, faster, or somehow better?

This is not a decision that can or should be made in a vacuum. The company has strategic goals, and marketing's activities should of course directly support those goals. Additionally, marketing's goals need to align with the revenue or operating model and with the customer engagement process via sales, support, and other customer-facing areas of the business. Because these models can vary widely, it is essential that marketing takes these into consideration when defining their own goals. A company that works only with Fortune 500 companies, selling multimillion-dollar deals with complicated and lengthy sales cycles, will have very different requirements from a local consignment store with six regional locations. Where and how your target audience gets their information will also be different, particularly if you are dealing with government customers, and should be taken into consideration when defining what marketing's goals will be.

Defining clear goals that are aligned with the organization at large is the first step in the process. Once those goals are established, it becomes possible to build the roadmap for your digital transformation.

Over the last five years, I have seen a definite shift toward revenue growth as to what companies expect from their marketing departments. Brand is still important, of course, as are things like corporate social responsibility and product marketing. But more and more, these and other more traditional marketing activities are being viewed through the prism of how they impact revenue. Are they creating organizational value, and if so, by how much? Marketing as a discipline is moving beyond vanity metrics toward providing concrete evidence of their contribution to value. The simplest way to do this is through demand generation—and then ensuring the other marketing disciplines are acting in concert.

That's why building a high-performance revenue engine to support top-line revenue growth is so important. Let's assume then that the goal of the marketing organization is to increase organizational value through the creation of top-line revenue. What is the best and most efficient way to deliver predictable revenue at scale? Who are the right people to source or train to build and run this engine? What skills do they need to have? Who do we hire first? How do I know if we have the right mix? Do we outsource or bring it in house? Where do we look to find the missing pieces?

And that's just the team members. What about the workflows and the processes? What do we need to start, stop, and continue doing to achieve this nirvana? What workflows are critical to marketing execution, efficiency, and accountability? Do we have these in place, or do they need to be implemented? And if so, how do we need to change them? What other parts of the organization do we need to align with, and how do we do that? What if they don't want to help? What should be the priority?

Finally, what technology do we need to invest in in order to build this machine? What are the core elements of this machine, and how do they work together? Can we use the systems we already have? How do we choose the right vendor for the job? What do we do if there is overlap in capabilities? Do we overinvest or make do with less?

These are but a few of the many questions you will need to address. However, this is not a simple how-to guide with every answer laid out in order. Digital transformation is not a prescriptive, plug-and-play initiative. However, this book will help you meaningfully frame the problem in light of your own unique context and situation, so you can make key decisions along the way—and, ultimately, develop an actionable plan that maximizes your chances of success. It won't be easy. It likely won't be pretty. But with dedication, determination, a lot of positive energy, and the help of this book, you will be able to realize the promise—and begin reaping the benefits—of digital transformation within your marketing organization.

PEOPLE, PROCESS, TECHNOLOGY

Digital transformation can only truly be realized by holistically managing the people, processes, and technology across the entire marketing spectrum. It can be captured with a helpful mnemonic that any business professional should appreciate: PPT. An approach balanced among these three key pieces will create an environment where the right people are doing the right things with the help of the right technology. Overinvestment in any one area will create bottlenecks or inefficiencies, and expectations will not be met. It's complicated, hard to do well, and can be intimidating. With all of that in mind, it helps to break it down into more manageable pieces and integrate those subsystems into the whole.

The team that you'll be asking to create this new paradigm is the most important component of embracing the digital transformation, and getting this right can make up for a lot of wrongs downstream. Assessing their existing skills and gaps, creating a balanced organization with the right type of expertise in the right areas, and putting in place a comprehensive training and coaching plan to ensure everyone is ready, willing, and able to tackle this challenge are critical steps. It goes well beyond finding experts on particular tools, instead focusing on the team as a unit. Like the "Miracle on Ice" US Hockey team of 1980, you don't need a stable full of superstars, but you do need people committed to their craft that are willing to be part of something larger than themselves. Those people are out there; it just takes a different approach to find them. And once you do, there will literally be nothing they aren't able to tackle.

As you're building the next great marketing team, you can simultaneously train your attention on the processes that they are using. The most important area to focus on is ensuring alignment with all stakeholders. This starts with agreeing on a single source of truth, creating a common set of definitions, establishing clear workflows, and setting expectations through service-level agreements. This is true for all internal processes contained within the marketing department but also extends to other groups, particularly sales, sales ops, and finance.

As you're constructing your team and defining your processes, it's time to incorporate the final element: the technology. Contrary to the beliefs of many, this is actually the simplest piece. It is relatively easy to identify which capabilities are needed and when in order to align with your overall objectives, capabilities, and timelines. The temptation is to solve the hardest problem first and overinvest in technology. But a measured approach that enables your team to properly implement, learn, and start seeing value from each incremental investment is generally the wisest path.

Where it gets complicated is choosing from over 8,000 marketing technology providers, each promising a silver bullet to solve your problems. It's easy to buy new technology that has overlapping capabilities with your existing systems or, even worse, to work at cross-purposes to each other. But focusing on what you need to do during every stage of your evolution can simplify this task considerably. That's not to say that it is easy to do, but it is the easiest of the three elements to execute and get right.

As you're probably starting to see, there is a lot to do, and even more to think about, in order to realize true digital transformation. It's a juggling act that requires coordination, discipline, determination, and at least a little faith. But I'm here to tell you that, if and when this transformation is done correctly, it's impossible to overestimate the positive impact the effort will have on your organization.

It does nothing less than fulfill all of the promises that marketing has been seeking to deliver to the business for the past 60 years: A nimble machine that can personalize messaging for every visitor, provide real-time feedback on the success and impact of these messages, and drive insight that powers adjustment to improve performance even further. It's a virtuous circle that continually improves your marketing ROI. It creates that data-driven, transparent revenue engine that delivers predictable revenue exactly when it's supposed to. That's not something we've enjoyed for the majority of marketing's existence, and it's something that we should all embrace.

Chapter 1

IT REALLY IS ALL ABOUT THE PEOPLE

Digital transformation is a tricky affair. Achieving any measure of success depends on many variables, but the most important of these are the people entrusted with the transformation. It is about more than just optimizing a generic marketing team. Digital transformation demands a different type of marketer altogether, someone uniquely suited to the ambiguity, accelerated pace, and at times unstructured environment of massive change. Building the right team means first finding the right players.

Championship teams don't happen by accident. Nobody ever won it all by grabbing the first few players they could find and throwing them into the fire. True greatness comes from the perfect balance of skills, attitude, desire, and sacrifice. It's rare that the best team is made up of the best individuals. Sure, there are individual superstars capable of doing extraordinary things, but teams composed entirely of these wunderkinds almost always underperform against expectations. The truly great teams operate as a cohesive unit where the strengths of the individuals are complementary, and their weaknesses are canceled out. It's a deliberate and painstaking process to find exactly the right combination, and only in very rare circumstances does it happen completely organically.

Arguably, one of the greatest examples of a perfect team is the 1980 US Men's Ice Hockey team. For anyone unfamiliar with the story, this hockey team was composed of a group of very young amateur hockey players, most of them college athletes, who somehow came together to defeat the Soviet Union—one of the greatest hockey dynasties of all time—at the 1980 Olympics, in Lake Placid.

To emphasize the point, the Soviets defeated the NHL All-Stars, a collection of some of the greatest individual hockey players on the planet, in a three-game series including a 6–0 shutout in game three, just a few months prior to the Olympics. This recent destruction of the elite professional ranks makes the US Olympic team's success that much more extraordinary.

How did a bunch of young and untested student athletes succeed where so many before them had failed? It wasn't their decades of professional experience or their world-class skills. This particular US team didn't have the world's best players. They didn't even have the best American players. What the US team did have was the right balance of specialized talent, a willingness to sacrifice themselves for the good of the team, a keen desire to win, and, perhaps most important of all, a coach that had a vision of what this team could accomplish.

The biggest challenge of all, and a testament to head coach Herb Brooks's greatness, is that he succeeded in getting the players to believe in themselves with the same conviction that he did. They bought into his vision of what they could be, they trusted each other, they believed in their coach, and they ultimately seized the opportunity to shock the world. I can still remember watching the game from my living room when I was 10 years old, not believing my eyes, and feeling a sense of pride and wonder that I couldn't describe—and really didn't understand. I just knew that I was seeing something important, something special, and to this day, I still get chills when I listen to the replay of Al Michaels's famous "Do you believe in miracles? YES!"

While it may be a cliché, achieving anything special always starts by getting the right people on board and believing. We've all been part of special teams; at work, in school, playing sports. At the time, it was probably hard to define what exactly about that team made it so special, but that didn't take anything away from it. It just worked. The individual members complemented each other, their skills meshed, and they were open and generous with their time and expertise. And more than likely, we had a good manager, teacher, or coach nurturing the environment and helping things along.

There are countless books on how to be a better leader, but that is not the purpose of this one. Truly transformational leadership comes from a lifetime of dedicated self-reflection and improvement, and if you want to be one of those, I'm afraid you'll have to look elsewhere for the secret code. I've also included some useful tools and templates in Appendix A if you're interested in a sneak peek. Now, let's discuss some guidance on the foundational elements to be considered when building a high-performance revenue generation engine.

ASSESSMENT

The first step of building your dream team is assessing your current team. Do the individuals have the right combination of traits to be effective not only in the desired end-state, but also during the often-tumultuous transition? To throw a metaphor into the mix, are they people you're willing to go into battle with—and that are likewise willing to join you? Finding these people is not that hard if you know which questions to ask. The hard part is identifying whether these key characteristics can be nurtured and cultivated in your existing staff—or will you need to make some hard decisions and find them outside your organization?

Taking inventory of existing team members is easy if everyone has been there awhile. Habits, experience, expertise, attitude—all of these things are laid bare over time and can be cataloged by an observant manager. Assessment is admittedly trickier when there isn't a long history of performance to refer to. If that's the case, it's important to solicit input from the extended teams. The best source for this crucial insight often comes from an individual's internal customers. Asking pointed questions about preferences and performance can expose both the good and the not so good in everyone. You'll need to rely on your own judgment as well—which, by definition, is subjective. To help you make better decisions, here is an order of operations for assessing your team that I've found useful over the years.

CURIOSITY AND DETERMINATION

First, you'll want to focus on two character traits as the foundational material for anyone on the team. Neither of them are dependent on experience or expertise but are, rather, naturally occurring tendencies. People either have them or they don't. And believe me when I tell you that for this journey you're going to want as many people as possible with the following traits. Whether inherited or sourced, those first two all-important traits to look for when building the team are curiosity and determination. Marketing as a discipline is rapidly evolving, and to keep up, the team needs to be naturally curious and equally determined if they are to keep pace. Here's why these are so important when it comes to making the digital transformation.

These traits manifest themselves in visible ways. Curious people ask a lot of questions. They are interested in why as much as how and never shy away from exposing their own lack of knowledge because the satisfaction of understanding is stronger than the fear of looking stupid. If someone has a reputation for challenging the way we always do things, that's a pretty good sign that they have the right attitude for digital transformation. Find more people just like them.

An innate desire to understand how things work, an insatiable drive to figure out why things happen the way they do, is 10 times more valuable than someone who knows which buttons to push on today's existing platform. By constantly asking questions, challenging the status quo, and searching for better ways to get things done, this skill set will never get stale. Someone who took apart their toys as a kid is preferable to someone with a decade of specific experience on a single tool. Specific experience is great until it's time to change, and if your team member doesn't care about figuring out what's next, they won't be able to keep up.

Determination is equally important. As today's marketing challenges get bigger, expand across more teams within the business, and become more critical to an organization's success, you're going to need people who can get things across the finish line. Because progress often takes a lot of work, those people that have a reputation for getting shit done are those that won't give up when things get hard—and believe me, when you go through a process like this, they will. The ability to fight through adversity, inertia, and yes, even nonsense, will be critical for seeing this transformation through to the end.

Likely, you will find fresh skills are required, new processes need to be established and optimized, and new tools need to be sourced, implemented, and used. Continuous improvement can feel like a never-ending game of Whac-A-Mole. To create efficiency out of the chaos, you need a determined and resourceful team, unafraid to tackle new challenges.

A recurring theme of any transformation is ambiguity. At any given moment, there will be lots of uncertainty as to what actually happened in the past, how things are being done today, and what's the right thing to do tomorrow. Curiosity and determination are perfectly suited to thrive in this environment. Tirelessly documenting and measuring progress while simultaneously identifying new and creative ways to evolve is incredibly satisfying to individuals with these personality types. The journey itself fuels their passion.

Put curiosity and determination together, and you've got an extremely powerful individual on your team. Pair them with someone similar, set the direction, and you'll be pleased with the results. Build your entire team of curious, determined professionals, and your job will be to create a vision and remove structural obstacles. Do that successfully, and there is no limit to what your team can accomplish.

A third characteristic, only slightly less important than the first two, is courage. Adding individuals brave enough to take measured risks, accepting the reality that they may fail, is also extremely important. Not everything will work during a transformation, and not everything should work. If everything always goes according to plan, chances are the plan is too conservative. But it takes a certain type of team member to willingly put themselves out there knowing it may not turn out as hoped. And yet, it's those types of people that turbocharge any transformation because they stress the system, which ultimately makes it stronger.

CULTURE FIT

The second thing to consider in assessing the existing or potential team members is culture fit. A happy-go-lucky team with a light and breezy attitude can make stressful situations seem less intense. A serious team that is all business can make quick work of challenging tasks. Neither is better than the other; they're just a little different in how they approach the work. Your job is to make sure everyone is willing and able to connect with the team's culture.

A number of years ago, I led a team that was formed during a merger of two companies. The cultures of the two teams were quite different, one fairly casual and the other more serious. Things got interesting when the new combined team started to develop a third culture that had elements of both, a result of the personalities mixing together. This new culture required a different approach from a leadership perspective in order to bring everyone together into a cohesive unit. The team visibly embraced the strengths of both approaches while being open to change, and I tried to model this flexibility in my own behavior.

It didn't stop with me, however, as it needed the individual team members to evolve as well. Those with the right attitude, regardless of skill set, had an advantage when it came to making this transition. Culture fit, while not exactly a hard science, is extremely important.

FINDING THEM

So how do you find people with these characteristics? The good news is, they're out there. The bad news is, we don't do a good job as leaders of asking the right questions in order to find them. Rather than asking for five or more years on this tool or specific experience with a certain activity, ask what books they read over the weekend or what their favorite subject was in school. And most importantly, be sure to ask *why*. You can tell a lot by the level of animation and passion in their responses. If their answer is a disinterested recitation of the latest corporate bestseller, YAWN. If they bounce in their chair with excitement as they share how their passions and interests have made them better at their jobs, don't let them leave until they sign a contract.

I once conducted an interview with a candidate for a customer marketing job. We spoke a little bit about the requirements and the job itself, but most of the conversation ended up being about how he recently ripped out all of the plumbing in his house and replaced it himself. Bingo! Curiosity! Determination! Courage! Nailed it.

CONSTRUCTION

Once you know you have the right type of person, you can work on finding the right balance of skills. Marketing as a discipline is broad and deep, and not everyone should have the same experience set. Continuing the hockey analogy, a team doesn't have 22 goalies. It's typical to have 12 forwards, eight defenders, and two goalies, because you need diversity among your players in order to compete effectively. The same applies for your marketing team.

An old boss of mine used to call work "pleasure with a purpose."

This philosophy has always resonated with me—as someone who invests a lot of my personal identity into my work—and I try to apply it to the teams I lead wherever possible. The point here is that, as a leader, you need to be conscious of bringing in pieces that will mesh. Digital transformation is hard enough without culture and personality friction, and getting the right type of people trumps the right skills nine times out of 10.

CORE EXPERTISE

Digital experts are going to be critical, but so are field and event marketers. Campaign and program experts are not the same as marketing operations professionals, but you're going to need both. Finding the right balance of skills is imperative to building the right team, so make sure you know what type of team you're building, and then hire accordingly.

What are those key areas to build first? You need digital expertise in the form of pay-per-click advertising, search engine marketing, and channel optimization, as well as a decent amount of website knowledge. You need a data analytics guru that can help you extract the insights hidden in all the data. You need marketing automation expertise, campaign and program managers, and field marketing pros to get started.

Digital marketing

Digital experts know how to build, execute, and measure digital marketing campaigns. They understand how ad platforms work, the strengths and weaknesses of each channel, how to manage a trade desk, how to segment audiences, and more. In short, they know how to push the right buttons to get the right asset in front of the right audience using the right channel. They may have some expertise in conversion-rate optimization and may even be able to do some elementary development work on the website. They understand how, when, and on what platforms to implement personalization. They can own the relationship with digital agencies (if the budget allows) and know how to minimize the cost of acquisition through bid and conversion-rate optimization. They take ownership of the digital investment across all channels and are responsible for improving this performance over time.

Working hand in hand with the campaign manager, they are responsible for optimizing the placement of the message in front of the right audience through the right channel for the lowest possible cost. They design and implement an execution plan to meet the lead and revenue objectives established by the campaign manager through continual improvement across all channels.

Web developer

The web developer may seem like a luxury, particularly for companies earlier in their evolution, but in my experience, the ability to proactively, efficiently, and *nimbly* manage the website is one of the most critical success factors for improving marketing performance. Your website is arguably your most important company asset—the front door to the world. Outdated, dysfunctional sites with confusing architecture, poor technical performance, or a bad user experience can be a significant drag on marketing's ability to generate revenue. It penalizes the site when the search algorithms rank for relevance. The value you'll receive from a developer on staff will more than exceed their fully loaded costs because they can quickly make updates, fix issues, and test and optimize journeys.

Some might respond that web development work is not a core competency and should be outsourced. While it's true the technical administration can be moved to a third-party vendor, do you really want to abdicate control of your most important company asset? In my mind, there is only one right answer to that question: a resounding NO. Between delays in getting even the simplest of updates made and the seemingly endless change orders and additional expenses, the opportunity cost of wasted time and agency management, as well as potential security and privacy risks, are all reasons to ensure you are in full control of your site.

Data analytics

Next, and this may come as a surprise to some, is a data analyst. Not a business analyst, someone who works on process or change management (although those are nice too), but a data analyst. This person connects disparate sources of data, aggregates the information, and creates visualizations that power data-driven decision-making. They are experts in spreadsheets and pivot tables but equally at home in visualization suites like Tableau or Looker. They know how to map data objects and can identify gaps or breaks in the data that may affect the quality of reporting.

Like a web developer, this may seem like a luxury and not really core to a marketing team's ability to generate revenue, but in fact, they are absolutely critical in uncovering the truth about a campaign and its overall demand generation performance. They create the dashboards that the rest of the team uses to improve performance over time, ensuring data quality and reporting integrity. The old axiom "You can't fix it if you don't know what's broken" is entirely appropriate here. If you don't know how your tactics are performing, how will you be able to improve them? You can't.

Ten years ago, measuring and tracking marketing's contribution with anything close to accuracy was extremely difficult, with a lot of manual processes and suspect technology. A lot has changed since then, and the challenge today isn't collecting and analyzing data so much as it is choosing which data to collect and analyze in order to answer key questions. Literally, there is almost nothing that can't be measured using today's tools, so judiciously choosing some key metrics that answer critical performance questions will be essential to scaling revenue. This is why the analyst is part of the core team that will deliver real value from digital transformation.

Marketing automation

Because automation plays such an important role in delivering scalable revenue, a marketing automation platform (MAP) expert is a required member of the core team. It doesn't matter which platform you're using, only that you have someone who knows how to maximize the utility of the tool. From landing page optimization strategies to sophisticated nurture campaigns, the ability to automate the execution of multiple programs simultaneously is a major contributor to improving throughput and performance without additional investment.

If there is an exception to the rule about hiring for culture before expertise, it would be here. The value of a certified expert on your MAP is hard to overestimate, and while it is always better if they have those desired traits and culture fit, getting a rock star to oversee and optimize the use of this critical platform can be a game changer.

Campaign management

The final member of the core team is a campaign manager. Someone who is both strategic and tactical is ideal because this is a very hard job to do well. They need to be able to work with sales and other marketing stakeholders to develop, from concept through execution, overarching campaign themes that resonate with your target audience. They need to be able to modify—and, in some cases, build from scratch—content for every stage of the buyer's journey. They need to be able to understand pipeline progression from first visit through closed-won. Finally, they need to be well versed in the other areas of demand generation, such as digital, web, automation, and analytics, to enable collaboration but, more importantly, to ensure their own strategies and tactics will be effective. They are the axle around which the rest of the teams revolve.

Remember, these are skills as opposed to individuals, so you don't necessarily need to start with a team of just five people. A large enterprise may have dozens of team members, a startup one or maybe two in each area. What is important is covering all five areas with a high degree of expertise.

These skill sets are also not mutually exclusive. For example, someone with web development skills can likely manage some basic data analytics work. Similarly, a campaign manager can learn how to use a MAP. Having said that, while there is a little overlap in some of these skills, each of these areas are complex enough (and important enough) that true specialization requires dedicated attention. At some point during the process, you will need to hire specifically for these skills, depending on your budget, available head count, and objectives.

Securing expertise in these five areas delivers the foundational elements required to build a marketing organization capable of delivering on the promise of digital transformation. As success grows and additional budget and resources are allocated to the team, you can expand the scope and start adding subspecialties. These might include account-based marketing experts, user interface or experience (UI/UX) specialists, additional resources for SEO (search engine optimization) and SEM (search engine marketing), and maybe even a content strategist. The sky is literally the limit once you have the engine in place.

The beauty of digital transformation is that it scales without the requirement of adding an army of new people. Additions like an account-based marketing expert can power a sophisticated program targeting a few to a few hundred named accounts for the cost of one full-time employee. The systems are in place to support this growth. The same is true for the other specialists, with one possible exception: events.

Offline trade shows are very time and resource intensive, and the ability to execute an event has little to do with the efficiencies created by digital transformation. This may not be an issue for your organization, depending on your investment strategy, but it's not unusual for companies to evolve relying heavily on events as a source of leads, and many find that habit hard to break.

As the company grows, and the expectations of marketing grow along with it, you can scale the team. Expanding into new international markets? Add some field or regional marketers to localize the content that the machine is generating. If you're spending more than $100,000 per month in digital advertising, it might make sense to bring that process and technology entirely in house by investing in a data management platform, a demand-side platform, and an expert to run them. Bottom line: Once you've got the core team in place, the rest is up to you.

There has been a lot written about T-shaped marketing

professionals, the notion that team members should be broadly versed in most of the subdisciplines of marketing while also having deep expertise in one of them. This is a useful model when building your digital transformation team. You should look for diversity in the wings of the T, so you have the right balance of experts and no single points of failure. This will provide management flexibility, room for personal growth among the team, and opportunities for advancement, and it will alleviate any pressure on you as the leader of having to be expert on every topic under the sun. It also frees you up to focus on evangelizing for the team during this transition.

TRAINING

For those current team members that have the requisite curiosity and determination to make this journey, it's important to build a profile for each that clearly identifies their skill set and their aspirations. Arguably, the aspirational part is more important than the skill set. Understanding where they want to take their career can provide valuable insight into how they might contribute to the success of this journey. Someone with moderate skills on a marketing automation platform may yearn to be a campaign manager. Similarly, an event's person may want to become more adept at visualization and reporting. It's your job as the leader to tease this information out of each and every team member so that a comprehensive strategy can be developed that meets the needs of both the business and the team.

Training is an essential ingredient for nurturing your good team into a great one. It also happens to be one of the easiest. It's about you being the coach that provides the time and space for them to acquire their new skills. Give the team access to attend a conference or tradeshow, provide access to online learning, buy training packages from your technology vendors. Investing in the skills of your team makes them better at their jobs, increases their emotional and mental engagement, improves loyalty to both you and the organization, and provides them with a platform for self-improvement that is extraordinarily valuable. That being said, this is not a free-for-all. Set expectations and timelines on training. What will be accomplished, by when, and how will it contribute to your team's and organization's overall goals?

I have purchased training credits from technology vendors for the entire team, good for unlimited sessions for an entire year, and only two of the six people took even a single class. They all wanted to, were grateful for the opportunity, but they never got around to it. I blame myself. I didn't provide them the necessary time and space to engage with the training, nor did I make it a priority. Consequently, the following year, we established completion dates and certification milestones and included them in their KPIs. Lo and behold, the courses were completed, and the new skills and expertise were integrated into our existing processes. It was a win–win.

Unfortunately, not everyone on the team is equipped mentally, intellectually, and even emotionally to take this journey. It is not for the faint of heart and will require fortitude and a willingness to sacrifice that not everyone is willing to invest in their work. An effective manager will know who they are by careful observation or by soliciting feedback from the extended teams. There is no shame for those individuals that are not willing to participate. It's not right or wrong. It is just a fact that some people will prefer to work in a more predictable and stable environment. For these people, I would recommend helping them find something else to do. These are always uncomfortable and challenging conversations, so it's important to always approach them with respect and empathy but be comforted by the fact that they would not be happy in the new environment. Helping them find something that is more to their liking ultimately is another type of win–win.

ONBOARDING

Finally, the third part of constructing your team is the onboarding process. Not only for new hires, mind you; this process must be applied to existing members of the team as well. Digital transformation is a journey that everyone is taking together. Things are going to change radically in some respects, with new expectations and challenges, and setting people up for success begins with onboarding.

Onboarding in this context covers setting expectations, establishing the new normal (which is even more important for existing team members than new ones), and ensuring everyone knows why we're undertaking this voyage. This is your chance to set not only the course for the team but to determine how it will develop. It's nothing short of creating the culture that will define the experience for everyone on the team. Will it be one where good enough is good enough? Will those that have been around for a while pine for the good ol' days, sapping the strength of conviction and making real change that much more difficult? Or will they be visible leaders, becoming enthusiastic supporters of the new vision?

The existing culture can be a significant roadblock to change; this sometimes boils down to a very simple sentiment: "That's not how we used to do it." It's innocent enough on the surface, but this mentality is insidious. It slows progress by erecting barriers, sapping momentum, and generally creating a stiff headwind that can be exhausting. Ironically, this mentality is not always the veteran's fault. It can also be a lack of vision and enthusiasm for change, and that falls squarely on the leader's shoulders.

For example, a company that had been in business for 45 years was experiencing a declining growth rate. Their revenue was still growing but at a slower pace every year. The leadership identified this as a problem and set about to change the trajectory through a combination of process and technology changes that leveraged the strengths of new tools to improve the volume of leads progressing through the funnel, the conversion rates between stages, and the velocity of opportunities to win.

What we didn't factor in was the inertia and the sense of complacency that consistently slowed our progress. However, it turned out that this wasn't due to laziness or a lack of tenacity among the team members; they simply didn't understand the desired future state or what was expected as part of the new normal. They wanted to turn around the decline but didn't know where we were headed or how to get there. In that confusion, they reverted back to old habits.

To combat this, we established a comprehensive program that outlined the overall goals, detailed the new changes (and why we were making them), defined what success looked like, and ensured every single team member—old and new alike—participated. It didn't fix the problem overnight, and there were some individuals that just didn't want to come along with the rest of the team, but for the most part, this solved the problem.

EMPOWERMENT

It's one thing to be told where you're going. It's quite another to be given the keys to the car. Just ask my 16-year-old. When you're the one making it happen, it stops being an academic exercise and gets real—real fast. It takes an incredible amount of trust, in both directions, to really deliver on the promise of digital transformation.

Leaders are not supposed to be experts in everything, but the team must have confidence in where they're going and know they have what they need to succeed. The team won't always know what to do, but their leaders have to trust that they have the skill, the desire, and the will to find a way. It's possible to create this dynamic, but again, it very rarely happens by chance. It takes a willingness to be a coach, provide air cover, and—most importantly—inspire the team by putting your own credibility on the line. Those willing to do those things can really increase the team's chances of achieving their goals. Here's what that looks like in practice.

BE A COACH

Every high-performance team has a good coach. In this context, I am defining a good coach as someone who is there for the team when they need guidance and support. It definitely is not someone who tells the team what to do. Using a sports analogy, most coaches of top professional leagues weren't all star players in their younger days. They may have played professionally, but more often than not, they were journeymen at best. This has given them a perspective different from those elite athletes because they had to struggle and adapt to remain relevant to their team. Their talent alone wasn't enough.

As coaches, this puts them in a better place than someone with otherworldly gifts. Mostly, this comes from the fact that not everyone can do what superstars were able to do as players.

LeBron James may struggle to teach someone how to play basketball at his level because, frankly, there are probably only two or three people on Earth that can do what he does. Telling someone to "just do what I do" isn't effective coaching and won't create a team of LeBrons that win championship after championship.

Where coaches earn their money, literally and figuratively, is by providing what their players need in any given situation. Juggling the needs of different personalities, all at different stages of the personal and professional evolution, creates all sorts of situations where a good coach can make a huge difference. At times, this may mean public acknowledgement for a job well done; at others, it may mean a private conversation on what could have been done better. It can take the form of tough love.

As a 14-year-old learning to play competitive basketball, I needed someone telling me exactly what to do. But as I matured, I needed that less and less. The best coaches I had found other ways to motivate and inspire. Talented managers I've had along the way recognized that fact as well and have acted accordingly. The best leaders rarely tell their team specifically what to do. They coach them along, asking insightful questions, probing for information, challenging team members to think through challenges on their own and come up with a proposed plan of action. This is appropriate not only for seasoned veterans but also for those just entering the workforce. The level of probing may be different, but asking questions and soliciting recommendations is effective no matter their tenure or experience level.

The leaders I've had in my career that were experts at this were far more valuable to my personal and professional growth than managers who just gave me the answer. I looked to them for guidance on where we were headed, what success looks like, and for resources to get the job done. It was on my shoulders to figure out the best way to do it. That is what I recommend to get the most out of your digital transformation. The technology is changing too quickly, the processes evolving seemingly overnight, which makes it impossible as a leader to be expert in all things for everyone. Be a good coach, provide the motivation and support, and then get out of the way.

AIR COVER

When you trust your team to figure it out, you're also putting a lot of pressure on them. It takes energy and time to carve a path through the proverbial jungle. They will need something from you if they are to be successful, and that's protection. It's the second key element of empowerment, and it is critical to digital transformation success.

Protection comes in many forms: protection from outside forces that threaten to distract from the tasks at hand, protection from scope creep, and protection from you. There will always be more work than time and people available to do it, and they need the power to focus.

A key element here is giving them the ability to say no—or, at the very least, to take something off the list every time something new gets added. I have worked for over two decades, and I have yet to see a case of this being implemented consistently and effectively, even by me. Again, this is my fault. As a leader, I have fallen victim to the desire to do more with less, to be all things to all people, however you want to say it. I've agreed to take on new responsibilities without checking with the team to see if there was bandwidth to cover it. I'm guilty as hell, which is why I am highlighting the critical importance of protecting your team. It can make a huge difference in the success or failure of your transformation.

The most effective teams are those that focus on the things that will make a significant impact and say no to those that won't. We've all been there. We've sat through annual and quarterly planning exercises and know what the strategic objectives are for the year. We leave the kickoff meetings all fired up, ready to go do those all-important tasks and really make a difference this year. That typically lasts through the end of the week, and then everyone starts getting consumed by the business-as-usual activities that constantly demand our attention.

The best way that I've found to combat this is to lead by example. The power to say no emanates from the top. If leadership asks you to take on something else, collaborate with your team to determine what can be sidelined. Resist the temptation to overdeliver by taking on more and more, instead embracing the fact that less, in many cases, is actually more. Five things done really well are often more meaningful than 20 done sort of ok.

Set the vision for the team, prioritize the objectives that will move the needle, and then spend most of your time protecting your team from the inevitable requests that will surface. It's not possible to deflect all of them, but do what you can to provide the team with the time and energy to focus on those things that will make a difference.

An important caveat here is that for this to work, the word *no* needs to be an acceptable answer coming from your own team. You may not agree, but you need to be willing to engage in that conversation for there to be mutual trust.

INSPIRE

The final factor of the people part of the equation is inspiration, and it is your responsibility to provide it. Consistent, enthusiastic, and optimistic reinforcement of the end-state nirvana is essential. Change is difficult under the best of circumstances, and a tireless evangelist of how great it will be will make a huge difference in both the velocity and the quality of the change. Evangelizing the movement happens on many levels.

First, and maybe most importantly, the individual needs to see how these changes will benefit them specifically. As a leader, emphasizing the personal benefits that come as a result of making this digital transformation can be a difference maker in getting that emotional investment the team will need to be successful. Job security, personal growth, easier workflows, a promotion, public recognition, any or all of these things may be instrumental in framing their perspective. If the individual team member can visualize these benefits and recognize their value, they will be an agent of change. The converse is absolutely true. If they see zero benefit from making the transition, they are unlikely to be a willing participant and the process is doomed. Consequently, make sure you're explaining the benefits in personal terms that everyone understands.

Second, there needs to be a well-defined benefit for the team. Will the marketing operations team be perceived in a new and better light as a result of the transition? Will the campaign team finally be recognized for their contribution? How does this transformation make the team look better to their peers, management, or the wider organization? Highlighting how these changes will improve the perception of the team can be a powerful motivator.

Next, how will marketing benefit? Will the department see additional investment if this all comes together? Will there be an opportunity to hire more people, get promoted, get more visibility at the company all-hands? What is that tangible benefit to marketing for getting this done?

And then finally, what does this do for the company? If marketing gets this right, do we get to initial public offering quicker? Do we increase our multiple for a private equity buyout? Will we get bonuses or raises? It doesn't always have to be monetary, but I've also never seen anyone turn down money, so that can be a useful tool. Just don't be blind to other methods of recognition as a way to inspire the team.

This inspiration can take many forms, of course, and you need to ensure that it's happening consistently, through multiple channels, to every individual. One-on-one meetings are excellent for sharing the vision of how this can improve an individual's quality of life; however, that is defined by them. Celebrating small victories and milestones is an incredibly powerful way to keep the team focused and engaged, and those celebrations can be fun and lighthearted as well.

At one stop in my career, I bought a trophy and engraved *Outstanding Contribution to the Field of Advancement* on the base. It was awarded peer-to-peer, every month, to someone who went over and above the call of duty. During the month, the winner could do whatever they wanted to the statue, as long as it wasn't permanently destroyed, and over time, it became quite a collection of quirky clothes, tattoos, and etchings. It was also highly coveted, and it was perceived as a real honor to be awarded this ridiculous object. It served as a visible reminder of what we were working toward and motivated everyone to keep the pressure on. Not bad for a $25 investment.

Assessing your team's strengths and areas for improvement, mapping out a plan to bring the right type together, and implementing a disciplined onboarding strategy are three powerful tools at your disposal to get the people part correct. Yes, it can be challenging, but with diligence and care, savvy leaders can find the right type of people to take on this perilous journey, confident they will have the fortitude and skills to deliver the value inherent in marketing's digital transformation.

Chapter 2

HOW $HIT GETS DONE

For many in marketing, process is a four-letter word. It's tricky and complicated, and there are lots of interdependencies that require a thorough understanding of the entire demand generation process. It requires a disciplined approach, as well as an open mind and a willingness to iterate over time. The simple fact is that it is an absolutely critical piece when it comes to realizing the benefits of digital transformation. Think of it as the plumbing for your house. It ensures there is running water, hot and cold on demand, showers, toilets, sinks—everything you need to maintain a healthy and convenient environment. It may not be interesting to talk about at parties, but the best plumbing is the kind that you never think about because you don't have to. However, someone needs to put all the pipes, valves, drains, and U-bends together in the first place to create that invisible yet important ecosystem.

A demand generation engine is no different. While getting the process correct is perhaps the least glamorous aspect of transforming the digital engine, it is critical. Some are intimidated by the complexity or unconvinced of the importance of establishing efficient processes. Marketers, in particular, often fall into this category because they mistakenly believe there isn't any creativity required to build good processes. There aren't exciting presentations with big reveals, no lunch meetings, no brainstorming sessions with whiteboards and crayons and snacks. There aren't focus groups with two-way mirrors where you spend an evening making snarky comments and eating pizza.

Most marketers believe that marketing is all about creating that important "Aha!" moment in our customer's consciousness. The creative inspiration that leads to the all-important engagement—that's the true purpose of marketing. Yes, we will follow the arcane and arbitrary rules set up by the operations team, but only because we have to. We're creatives, dammit, and process is the one thing standing between us and bringing our ingenious, inspired ideas to the masses.

That's where they would be wrong. Designing, implementing, and optimizing good processes is a wonderful opportunity to flex creative muscles. Redefining legacy workflows, eliminating bottlenecks, increasing throughput, and accelerating deliverables are all opportunities ripe for improvement that contribute real efficiency gains and create organizational value. Even better if they are developed collaboratively with other marketing teams and extended stakeholders. A good process needs to work for everyone, and there are plenty of situations where a simple process had to be revisited multiple times because key stakeholders had been left out of the design process. Good marketers build good marketing processes. Great marketers build great organizational processes and take responsibility for getting it done.

The historic abdication of this key responsibility for documenting, adhering to, and improving internal marketing processes has contributed to the perception that marketing as a discipline is not scientific or predictable. One of my favorite *Far Side* cartoons of all time shows a scientist at a whiteboard. There is an equation on the far left, the answer on the far right, and, in the middle, an amorphous cloud tagged with the words *A Miracle Happens.* If that were only true. Alas, process is a critical component of getting digital transformation right, for marketing and for every other discipline. It has only taken us marketers a little longer to figure that out.

So what does process actually look like in practice? In fact, what *is* process in the first place? Simply put, process is the physics of business. It is the set of rules that define the system, govern how tasks progress and interact, and ultimately, how things perform. Anyone with more than 15 minutes' worth of professional experience will tell you that the mechanics of how things get done depends on many things, some logical, some not so much. Some processes were developed as a path of least resistance. Some were created based on personal preference. Some come as a result of vendor recommendations or system requirements, while others fall into the dreaded category of "We've always done it this way."

Regardless of how you arrived at your current state, your processes—and at times, the lack of one—govern how marketing does its business. These established workflows are either helping or hindering your ability to execute. In some cases, no process at all may in fact be better than the one currently in place. When processes are not meeting the needs of the situation or even actively slowing things down, teams will either ignore them or build workarounds to get the job done. It's critical that you evaluate your current processes to ensure they are supporting your organization's need to transform digitally and meet your overall goals. But where do you focus your efforts, and how do you get started?

Scalable revenue generation that is predictable and transparent is not possible without first ensuring these four crucial parts:

- A single source of truth
- Common definitions
- Clear workflows
- Agreed-on service level agreements

ESTABLISHING A SINGLE SOURCE OF TRUTH

A single source of truth is exactly what it sounds like. It's the baseline data that everyone agrees is real. You may have heard the phrase "Lies. Damn Lies. And Statistics." It means that data can be used selectively—and even manipulated—to tell literally any story whatsoever. If two different groups within your organization are using data points from two different sources, there is a high likelihood that they'll have different interpretations and predictions. And that's a problem.

Digital transformation can solve that problem by leveraging the power of the sales organization's core technology that powered their own transformation a decade ago. Stitching together what happens on the marketing side of the fence with what happens on the sales side is absolutely critical in order to achieve revenue generation at scale. It is the connection point that unites both organizations and creates true synergy from prospect to renewal and every step along the way.

In practice, marketing and sales often use different systems for reporting, and consequently, they rarely agree on the conclusions drawn from the data. Under the best of circumstances, this leads to confusion. Under the worst, it leads to suspicion and a lack of trust that erodes the ability to work together constructively. "Marketing doesn't give us any good leads" is a common complaint I've heard throughout my career. In the other direction, marketers like to disparage sales's ability to close deals from the leads they provide. When the two groups are using different data sets, it's easy to create an environment where both sides feel they are right and the other is wrong. It's an atmosphere that leads to tension and inefficiency and is one of the most destructive forces that can impact any revenue generation team.

The best way to alleviate this tension is to agree to use a common system—a single source of truth—for any given set of data. Only then can each group be confident that the data they're using won't be called into question by anyone else.

Connecting sales and marketing is an obvious example, but a lack of consistency in the data can impact teams within marketing as well. If one arm of the team is using Basecamp or some other project management system, while another group is using a homegrown system, confusion and inefficiency will result. It may not give rise to acrimony, as it often does between sales and marketing, but it is still a serious issue that must be addressed. The important part is that teams align around and agree to work within the guardrails of a single system.

It's clear that a single source of truth is the best medicine when it comes to eliminating this tension. However, in the early stages of digital transformation, this may not be entirely possible. In most marketing organizations, before they achieve higher levels of maturity, data is collected and stored literally all over the place. Personal contact information resides in the marketing automation platform, while visitor and cookie data is collected by your website analytics platform. Security and privacy rules may necessitate a third-party data management platform to ensure compliance. Finally, information relating to deal stage, size, and velocity, as well as account and contact data, is being stored by sales in the CRM (customer relationship management) platform.

There isn't much reason to doubt the need to use the CRM as the primary data source for measuring pipeline generation effectiveness, for example. Responders, leads, and prospects are all important and interesting to marketers, but until they convert to qualified leads, opportunities, and eventually wins, sales is right to be mostly disinterested. Consequently, it's fine as a marketing organization to spend a lot of your time and energy in the marketing automation platform (MAP), adding prospects and leads to the database and nurturing them through the journey. However, making the all-important connection between that MAP and the CRM should be a top priority.

Without this connection, it is impossible to connect marketing's efforts to revenue. It's also impossible to perform sophisticated channel optimization, because while minimizing the cost per acquisition of a lead is important, if you're using more than one channel to generate leads, you're going to need to know the conversion rate from lead to opportunity for each one of those channels. Otherwise, you may wind up optimizing for the wrong things.

Because of this reality, you may have to create a single source of truth in stages. The first step will be to get marketing's house in order, and that starts with your MAP. The majority of your lead data is collected and stored in the MAP. This is good news because these systems typically have robust management capabilities and sync nicely with CRM platforms. For a revenue engine, this synchronization point is absolutely critical; this is where the outbound marketing activities are connected to pipeline opportunities. And here's the key: Marketing must be present where sales lives.

As one example, at a former company, we connected our MAP (Marketo) to our CRM (Salesforce) and set up the synchronization to happen every night at midnight local time. We weren't making any decisions in a time frame of less than a day, so it didn't make sense to give the extra effort to build a real-time sync. Our reporting and decision-making were structured on a 24-hour cycle time, so it was important to get that nightly sync and push the data out to the edges of the network.

Importantly, we worked closely with our sales ops team to establish the sync cadence, and everyone was aligned on both the timing and the data that was being shared. Any subsequent report or decision based on this data was therefore credible and accepted by both teams. If Salesforce said we passed 25 qualified leads to the business development reps (BDRs) yesterday, everyone agreed that 25 leads were added to the queues. There was no shade to hide in—a critical win for all concerned.

It's important to pause here to mention that the measurement—and, therefore, the life—of a sales professional is binary. Every 90 days, they are issued a pass/fail grade based on the quarterly performance. The method used to assign these grades is the data residing within the CRM system, and they live and die by that system. As a marketer, if you want your data to be not only accessible but also credible in the eyes of sales, it must live in the CRM. That's the single source of truth.

With that in mind, as you look to define and refine your processes to realize the full benefits of your digital transformation, job number one is to connect the MAP to the CRM and sync it as often as possible. The situation on the ground can change quickly, so monthly synchronization isn't going to cut it. Even weekly syncs are likely not often enough. In the other direction, real-time synchronization is probably a waste of time and energy. When the data is fresh, resides in a shared repository, is accessible to everyone, and serves as the foundation of all reporting, you have the functional capability to generate revenue at scale. It is a hard, but essential, first step, and ultimately will eliminate a lot of tension, disagreement, and poor decision-making downstream.

COMMON NOMENCLATURE

Getting everyone to use the same data platform is no small feat, and it's only the first step in real process optimization. Equally important is creating a set of definitions and socializing them with the extended teams, both internal and external to marketing, to come to an agreement on exactly what is meant at every stage of the sales cycle. There are two dimensions to this process, those within the marketing team and those with other parts of the business. Let's tackle the internal ones first.

NAMING CONVENTIONS WITHIN MARKETING

In order to build a scalable revenue engine, there need to be logical taxonomies to the channels, programs, and the website. This includes assigning consistent names and values for every marketing activity you pursue. It sounds intimidating, but it isn't really. It means building a logical structure that assigns variables to those data points you need to capture to measure performance and make decisions. For example, if you hope to optimize your marketing programs' spending only between offline and digital activities, your taxonomy only needs to accommodate offline versus digital channels. However, if you plan to optimize spending within multiple digital channels (which I would strongly recommend!), such as Google versus Bing, you'll need to create a variable that enables you to distinguish between those activities. The important point here is to measure as deep as is required to make critical decisions. If you're not going to use the data as part of the optimization process, don't collect it. One important caveat is that, if you plan to act on it later, even if you aren't doing so today, still record the data. Retroactively changing these systems creates challenging discrepancies in your existing data, or you may lose the historical perspective and be forced to analyze data from this point forward only.

Digging deeper, for outbound tactics, the first piece is naming your campaigns, programs, channels, sources, and mediums. This powers the creation of what is called an urchin tracking module, or UTM. The name isn't that important, but the UTM itself is the foundation of all reporting. They are unique codes that can be attached to your digital outbound tactics. These codes are then captured by your landing page, which identifies exactly where this particular visitor is coming from. The MAP manages these codes, mapping the source to a prospect and creating a one-to-one relationship between that tactic and the individual. Further integration with the CRM allows the savvy marketer to track performance of individual tactics all the way through to closed-won.

UTMs are literally the keys to the kingdom when it comes to optimizing marketing investment across all tactics, and it only becomes possible when you have a taxonomy that identifies all the different variables and creates a systematic way of managing all of them. There are any number of excellent resources on UTMs, their importance, their use cases, and how to create them. I've included a few links and resources in Appendix B if you're interested in learning more about them. The important point here is that you need a naming convention that can scale as your programs become more sophisticated.

It is also vital that you build with an eye toward the future. You may have more modest capabilities today, focusing on a few channels like display advertising and offline events. But with any luck, you will soon have an increased budget for additional channels, and your marketing definitions and naming convention need to be able to accommodate that growth.

There is a real science to this that, when done well, can be a true differentiator for the entire demand generation function. Building a comprehensive taxonomy that reflects the current requirements but can also accommodate additional tactics and improvements in the future is perhaps the core element of success for the entire engine. It's why I said the one exception to the hiring rules is finding that marketing automation platform expert; they can build for today and tomorrow, as well as enforce the rules that are established. Getting this part right ensures that the data reflect the truth in what is enjoying success in the market and allows for continual optimization over time. Getting it wrong results in garbage in, garbage out, and you'll never achieve true channel optimization.

DEFINITIONS FOR THE LARGER ORGANIZATION

Establishing common definitions within the marketing team is critically important, but equally important is agreeing on shared language among other parts of the business. First and foremost is working with the sales and sales ops teams to ensure there are consistent definitions for the various stages of the buyer's journey, including visitors, contacts, responders, prospects, leads, qualified leads, and opportunities. It is impossible to overstate the importance of getting this alignment. The second component is clarity on the criteria for advancing from one stage to the other. The point of the first is to make sure everyone is using common language in describing the funnel. The point of the second is to get concurrence around how it works. Failure to do either of these things results in problems.

A frequent source of tension between marketing and sales has historically been confusion—and often disagreement—around what constitutes a lead. Marketing might define a lead as someone who has completed a form or attended a webinar or even an in-person event. They have engaged with some content, showed some level of interest, maybe even intent, and are willing to speak to someone about a possible solution to their pain. In short, they have traded personal contact information in exchange for something of value, and marketing may think that their work here is done. Sales, on the other hand, may believe a lead is someone who has engaged with a lot of content, has compared their solution to other competitors, has decided to move forward with their company, and needs someone to help them purchase the solution. Both definitions are valid, but they are clearly not congruent. This divergence of definition often adds to the lack of trust and overall friction between sales and marketing.

With this in mind, here are some suggestions that can serve as the basis for defining these terms within your organization. As with everything else, there is room for customization for your unique situation, but these should go a long way in helping you get that much-needed alignment between the teams.

Target

A *target* is an individual that meets some minimum set of requirements for inclusion in marketing's addressable audience. Industry, job title, company—there are lots of data points that can trigger inclusion in marketing activities. What they are specifically depends on how your organization defines the market, and you should align sales, marketing, and senior leadership around a common definition. But it's important to understand that a target is merely someone within this selection set.

Responder

A target that has engaged on any level with one or more marketing activities is a *responder*. They may have clicked an ad and visited your website, arrived via a search engine or another site, clicked on a link in a third-party email, or any other action that signifies intent. At this stage, they have not yet submitted their contact information but could still be identifiable. A common example of this is when a website visitor gets identified by their device cookie (and is recognizable by the system when they return).

Lead or prospect

A *lead* or *prospect* is an individual that has engaged with a marketing activity, either yours or a partner's, and whose personal contact information has been collected. They may have completed a form on the website, registered for a webinar, or stopped by the booth at a tradeshow. Whatever the channel, the important thing is that you have some personally identifiable information that they have voluntarily given to you or to a third party you work with. They have shown some intent but have not yet engaged in the type of behaviors that would advance them to a status of a qualified lead.

Marketing qualified lead (MQL)

An individual that has accumulated enough points through engagement to signal buying intent has been *qualified* by marketing. This point threshold is an agreed-on but somewhat arbitrary amount that the team collectively believes represents genuine buying intent. In other words, any individual that achieves this status has a higher propensity to convert into an opportunity and is therefore the subject of greater focus and investment.

This status can be achieved by completing multiple activities, such as repeated website visits or content downloads, or by completing a single task like requesting to speak with a sales representative. What's important is that everyone agrees they have done enough to warrant sales outreach.

Sales accepted lead (SAL)

A sales accepted lead is when the sales team has agreed to pursue an individual. This is where the rubber meets the road, the critical juncture between marketing and sales, when both teams agree a lead is worth applying sales resources to. There isn't necessarily much of a difference between MQL and SAL from a pipeline value standpoint, but it is critically important to measure and optimize this conversion rate. If the conversion rate is low, it suggests that there are different expectations between what marketing and sales believe is a sales-ready lead. This disconnect can be the source of a lot of tension between the teams and is easily reconciled by agreeing on standard definitions.

Opportunity

An *opportunity* is an individual that has progressed to the point where sales is willing to fully engage with and be measured on the outcome. Typically, this means identifying the primary contact within an account, quantifying the deal size, defining a purchase time frame, and establishing other meaningful attributes of an anticipated deal. It's not necessarily the first stage in the CRM, nor does it have to be. Again, depending on the sales cycle and revenue model, classifying an opportunity may not come until quite late in the sales process. The important part is getting agreement on the definition of an opportunity and the minimum criteria it must meet.

While this is not necessarily a comprehensive list of all possible stages of the buyer's journey, it should be a good start to bring transparency and accountability to the revenue engine. It may be tempting to overengineer the sales pipeline by adding additional stages, but that is typically a fool's errand. Unless you will make decisions or investments based on those additional stages, the additional complexity outweighs any reporting fidelity you may extract, particularly if you allow nonstandard progression through the stages (e.g., stage skipping or fishing). Once progression benchmarks have been established for every stage in the pipeline, you can begin the important work of optimizing conversion rates from one to the next.

The only way to eliminate the conflict is to create definitions of what exactly is meant by each of these terms. When that subjectivity is removed, the only thing left to talk about is volume and velocity.

CLEAR WORKFLOWS

What most people think of when they hear the word *process* is workflow, the path objects take as they progress through a system. How a web visitor becomes a lead, which then progresses to an opportunity and then becomes a customer, is an example. The approval chain for a press release is another. Like an interstate highway system, workflows connect destinations using defined pathways that are optimized for speed, efficiency, and convenience.

What makes them particularly important when pursuing digital transformation is that they power scalability. Documenting and benchmarking your workflows against industry best practices helps to identify bottlenecks, streamline production, and reduce timelines. It is the core element to your continuous improvement program and allows you to deliver greater efficiency over time—the proverbial "do more with less."

Because workflows are literally everywhere, from content production and review processes to launch schedules and event execution, it is easy to be intimidated by the size and complexity of optimizing them all. However, you do not need to do them all at the same time. It's ok to prioritize some of them, delay or even sunset others, all based on the immediate needs of the demand generation engine.

The two workflows that have the largest impact on this topline growth are your lead scoring and lead passing processes. Getting these two correct is the difference between predictable and transparent demand generation and a collection of feel-good activities that may or may not be contributing any real value to the organization.

A number of positive outcomes result from well-defined, clearly documented, and efficiently executed lead scoring and lead passing workflows. It helps to reduce functional and reporting errors. It increases the quality of leads being delivered to the sales teams. It creates accountability chains, identifying where there are gaps or opportunities for improvement. It accelerates onboarding of new team members in marketing, sales, and sales operations and reduces the impact of turnover or territory restructuring. Most importantly, it allows an organization to scale, because it quantifies exactly how things progress through the systems and exposes capacity gaps that result in resources sitting idle. For example, documenting the lead passing process may reveal a huge surplus of leads that are sitting in lead queues because there aren't enough sales development reps (SDRs) to follow up with all of them. The reverse may be true as well, with not enough leads coming through to feed the number of SDRs. In either case, resources are sitting idle, and that's inefficient. That being said, lead scoring and passing optimization are perhaps two of the least glamorous aspects of revenue generation, but they're arguably some of the most important. Let's take a look at how you get these right.

LEAD SCORING

For the uninitiated, lead scoring is the assignment of "points" for various activities and behaviors a prospective customer undertakes. To illustrate, let's say that the marketing, sales ops, and sales teams have all agreed that a contact that has accumulated 100 or more points can be promoted to the inside sales team as a qualified lead.

There are lots of different ways an individual can accumulate these points. Downloading a white paper may earn them 20. Visiting several product pages in a 72-hour time frame may earn them another 20. Clicking on a recorded demo may give them 50 points, and they may get an additional 25 if they watch that video through to completion. Completing a form that requests a meeting with someone in sales or a live demonstration may award them 100. Regardless of what they did or how quickly they did it, the important milestone is the accumulation of 100 points.

The number of points assigned should not be arbitrary and needs to be customized for each individual company. It doesn't really matter what the point values are; what matters is that you define and implement a strategic approach that allocates points according to demographic data points, desired behaviors, the value of those behaviors, and the eventual outcomes tied to those behaviors.

It is also important to remember that these scoring models are not—and should not be—poured into concrete. Changing the values is a straightforward exercise in nearly every MAP on the market. It's entirely possible, and recommended, to use A/B testing when rolling out a scoring system. Implement a change based on the best available information and measure the results for 60 days. Some adjustments may be immediately obvious, either for better or for worse, but I encourage you to stick with any existing model for at least two months. That way, you're likely eliminating any seasonal or other temporary influences that may be occurring.

One change I can suggest without hesitation is to implement some form of funnel-based scoring into your model. This is nothing more than allocating more points to engagement with bottom-of-funnel assets when compared with top-of-funnel. At the beginning, these values will necessarily be guesses or assumptions about the intent behind those actions and behaviors, and that's ok. A thought leadership white paper, for example, is a useful asset for someone who is still trying to define their pain point. They need the high-level contextual information but aren't yet comparing individual vendors or pricing potential solutions. Assets such as these should be worth fewer points than a white paper that has in-depth comparisons of competitors' offerings. Careful observation over time will reveal which assets lend themselves to the various stages, at which point adjustments can be made. In this fashion, you're building a machine that accelerates those that are ready to talk turkey and those that are still kicking the tires.

Another temptation to resist is basing your scoring model on the format of content delivery, or channel. White papers are not automatically top-of-funnel assets. Similarly, webinars are not always bottom-of-funnel. In this case, as in many others, the content is king, and your model should reflect this reality.

Because lead scoring exists in your MAP, as do your nurture capabilities, it's quite simple to create a sophisticated and efficient strategy for progressing prospects from the top of the funnel to the bottom and then on to sales. Additionally, over time, patterns will emerge that can be exploited to your benefit. If you observe that prospects who engage with a certain asset (an ROI calculator, for example) tend to convert at a higher rate, you may want to increase the point value for that specific asset to see if you can convert them more quickly.

In our original system, a prospect that registered for our recorded webinars, regardless of topic, was given a point value of 35. In the new model, webinar topics were categorized based on buyer intent, and contacts were awarded greater point values for engaging with a webinar that corresponded with high intent (such as product demos) than those that corresponded with low intent (such as thought leadership webinars). As it turned out, we were getting a lot of registrations for our product demo webinars, and our hypothesis was that attendance at these webinars was a sign of high intent relative to our thought leadership or educational webinars. We adjusted the model such that those that registered for a product demo webinar received 70 points, and someone who clicked on a thought leadership webinar collected the original 35 points.

We observed a number of things as a result of this test. First, we saw a measurable increase in the volume of qualified leads. Great information, and that alone was worth executing the change. And we also noticed a significant increase in the conversion percentage of those leads into opportunities. This confirmed our hypothesis that engaging with this type of bottom-of-funnel content was a true intent signal and that these prospects were ready to engage with the sales team.

The strategy behind the change was discussed over the course of several weeks, where we developed our hypothesis and the method of testing. The actual change in the system literally took us a couple of hours to implement. The result was more leads and higher conversion rates to opportunity. It was a classic win–win and something that we continued to refine over time. I recommend revisiting the scoring model once a quarter to ensure it is still performing as designed, as well as to test new hypotheses aimed at continued optimization and improvement. As your confidence and sophistication grow, so will your appetite for testing. Taking a more holistic view across the entire sales cycle, from first visit through closed-won, can provide second-order insight to drive further improvements. For example, identifying what content was consumed most frequently and when by your MQLs and opportunities will unlock new nurture ideas that can really accelerate revenue. The sky's the limit when you've got the process in place to continually improve.

There is no reason to wait to implement a lead scoring system or to improve the one you already have. Remember that perfect is the enemy of the good. Any lead scoring system is better than none, and by constantly revisiting the performance and outcomes, it won't take long before you have an optimized and efficient scoring model that is delivering tangible value.

LEAD PASSING

As you define your lead scoring strategy and implement a continuous improvement process, you can simultaneously outline your lead passing workflow. It is doubly important here to ensure you are working hand in glove with the sales ops and sales teams. Lead generation engines often break down at this critical juncture, where the lead is passed from marketing to sales, because there are a number of forces at work that are difficult to account for completely.

Lead passing, similar to lead scoring, can be very simple or incredibly complicated. There is no right answer for everyone, but there is a right answer for your organization. There are technical issues to contend with, ensuring data is synchronizing as expected and on time, processes may not be aligned due to competing objectives, and there are personalities and experience levels that need to be managed. None of these issues is insurmountable in and of itself, but taken together, they can cause havoc.

Inside sales rep and BDR teams typically suffer from high turnover. It's a very difficult job—high pressure, typically with few of the benefits enjoyed by more senior account executives. These teams usually have dual purposes, tasked with following up on any and all inbound leads, as well as carrying some quota for outbound activities. They're extraordinarily busy, pulled in multiple directions, and operate at a critical yet delicate juncture in the sales pipeline.

As such, it's marketing's responsibility to ensure there are clearly defined rules about what constitutes a qualified lead, which we've already discussed, but also to commit to routing them appropriately. There are many different strategies available for routing the leads, with pros and cons to each. Leads can be passed by industry, geography, deal size, or based on any number of criteria. I don't have a particular favorite; it really depends on the revenue model, sales cycle length, territory maps, organizational philosophy, and—honestly—on whatever approach the chief revenue officer is most comfortable with. There's nothing wrong with any of these models; what's important is that there is a defined workflow, and that marketing adheres to it.

I recommend not only working with the sales operations team, but actually partnering with them as joint owners of the router. As we previously discussed, sales turnover can be rampant, and territory maps may change frequently—so unless marketing is part of the decision-making process (and they usually aren't!), confusion, delays, and errors in lead routing will be inevitable. By having joint ownership of the router, many of these issues can be averted.

Similar to the lead scoring model, I recommend a regular checkpoint be scheduled every 90 days or so to ensure the process is up to date and functioning as desired. Going more than a quarter without a review runs the risk of inefficiency and lost revenue. First, with the turnover and fluidity of coverage maps, going longer than a quarter without a review means that some queues may go dark. If leads are still being passed to people no longer on the team, no one is going to follow up. Best case, the prospect completes another form once the dead end has been removed, and you've lost nothing but time. Worst case, the lead became frustrated because their queries went unanswered and turned to a competitor. At that point, marketing dollars and time have been wasted or even created demand for someone else. Ouch.

Second—and this happens more often than you think—errors crop up in the system that cause all kinds of headaches. There is an opportunity cost when a BDR is fixing problems in the queue and is performing lead passing hygiene. When they're spending their time identifying and reporting errors, they're not calling prospects. It also causes confusion when leads are assigned outside of the normal and defined process, as reps may believe there was a change in policy when none occurred.

Third, and most damaging, leads may go missing. In any highly competitive market, it's important that no lead gets left behind. Not many companies can afford to leave revenue on the table, and unmonitored lead queues are exactly that. Not only that, but it also erodes much needed trust among marketing, SDRs, and sales and damages marketing's credibility. Consequently, it's in marketing's and sales's best interest to ensure anyone who raises their hand gets a call. I remember an instance where we discovered over 3,000 leads in a queue that no one was monitoring. This amounted to over 20% of our annual lead volume. Needless to say, it was disappointing on many levels, and since then, I've never again gone more than 90 days without checking the lead passing process.

Next, I recommend a weekly cadence with your SDR team. This meeting serves two purposes. It ensures that the lead routing is working smoothly and as expected. If leads are appearing in the wrong queue or, worse yet, not appearing at all, this weekly checkpoint will catch such issues before they become serious problems. Such a meeting also provides a forum for other important matters, such as quality checks on the leads themselves, confirming funnel stage definitions are well understood and being appropriately applied, and ensuring compliance with the SLAs.

A monthly meeting with sales leadership is also a very good idea. It provides a forum for validating the processes are working as expected, the quality of leads is sufficient, and generally reinforces the alignment between the two teams. This meeting should include the CMO, the CRO, the leader of the sales ops team, and the demand generation lead. Depending on how your sales team is organized, you may want to include sales leaders if it makes sense, as well as the head of the inside sales team. Who attends is something to be determined jointly with sales and sales ops, including those that can add value to the discussion, but scheduling and maintaining a monthly meeting to validate that the machine is working is critical to success.

SERVICE LEVEL AGREEMENTS

The last process that is fundamental to digital transformation is creating and meeting service level agreements (SLAs). SLAs are defined as a contract between supplier and customer, laying out a defined set of tasks or deliverables and, importantly, a time frame for completion. In short, it's a commitment to take action within a specified time frame. SLAs are critical to the efficiency and predictability of the revenue generation engine and therefore needs to be a top priority.

SLAs can be applied within the marketing team to ensure certain obligations are met. Review timelines, production schedules, creative updates, campaign execution, and other marketing activities all lend themselves to agreed-on time frames for completion by various team members. Any marketing organization that wants to improve throughput needs to consider SLAs for these and other internal processes. However, in this context, the most important SLA to implement is the lead follow-up SLA.

The decay rate of leads is fast. It's very fast. Consequently, it's important to align around a defined lead follow-up program that minimizes the time elapsed between marketing qualifying the lead and the SDRs' first-touch follow-up. This is not only to ensure the minimization of leads getting stale but also to serve as a vehicle to measure individual performance and identify areas for improvement.

This step isn't as straightforward as it may appear on the surface. It's easy to establish an SLA that feels right; it's as simple as defining it. But a lead in the system is a human being, and that individual is living their life according to their own unique schedule and commitments. Their entry into your lead queue is one small event from their perspective—if they're even aware of it at all—and their ability to pick up the phone or answer an email may not coincide with your SDR's planned outreach. It is impossible to overstate the importance of establishing expectations for lead follow-up. It is a critical component of any digital transformation effort for two important reasons.

First, SLAs are the most efficient vehicle to bring about personal accountability. It is easy to recognize that reporting on individual performance metrics is fraught with political peril. Most people would rather not have their performance publicly scrutinized on a daily basis; someone will inevitably be at the bottom of the list, and nobody wants to be that person. Recognizing that shining a light on individual performance carries emotional baggage and can lead to morale or other issues, it's important to treat this action with respect and candor. With careful messaging and consistent application of rules, measuring and reporting at the individual level can be an effective tool for achieving insight and improvement. By consistently showing that those who are meeting—or, better yet, exceeding—their SLAs typically have better results downstream can be very motivating. The goal is not to embarrass or punish, although some will perceive it as such. Rather, at its core, it is about setting expectations and creating predictability through transparency and accountability.

Second, measuring the velocity throughout every stage of the funnel is the only way to establish a predictable sales cycle. The time to first touch is no exception—and it may, in fact, be one of the most critical factors influencing conversion to opportunity. The fact that lead follow-up is measured in the aggregate provides some leeway at the individual level to accommodate for special circumstances. No one should be reprimanded for any single lapse. But setting the expectation that lead follow-up happens within a defined SLA is a useful metric that can be used to improve overall pipeline performance, either through process or quality improvements or through personal efficiency and accountability changes. With this in place, it's possible to work backward from deal closure to understand how long it takes for buyers to progress through the entire pipeline. Without this key metric, marketing's contribution is still subjective and therefore not truly transformative.

The process, because it's documented and agreed on by all involved parties, is the inner workings of the engine driving your demand generation. It is a blueprint that can be optimized for increased performance, providing a consistent platform that can scale up and down as resources are added or constrained. The machine is capable of scaling quickly because there is clarity on what happens, when it happens, and who initiates it. Resource planning becomes a strategic decision, as opposed to a haphazard exercise.

Chapter 3

TECHNOLOGY TO HELP YOU SCALE

Today's marketers are the same earnest, hard-working, dedicated professionals as their parents a generation earlier. Processes come and go as different people with different perspectives figure out different ways of getting the job done. What has really changed over the past decade is the technology. At times, the capabilities available to today's organizations seem almost unbelievable, with the ability to target specific individuals and create a dynamic, customized experience based on their unique profile. It really is the technology that has accelerated this transformation and created so much value, for both the client and the vendors.

So much so that more than 8,000 marketing technology (MarTech) providers are providing today's marketers with the power and insight to treat every single individual in a highly targeted and personalized manner. For sci-fi fans, you may remember the movie *Minority Report* and its representation of the retail environment in the year 2054. Tom Cruise's character goes to the mall, and as he's walking past storefronts, personalized messaging appears on multiple screens. Through facial recognition and data mapping, the retailer knows who he is, his purchase history, and his likes and preferences and is able to craft personalized messages in real time and deliver them through multiple engagement points to drive sales.

The movie, though dystopian, provides a glimpse of what has been the holy grail for marketers since, well, forever. Marketing, as a discipline, has been marching steadily in this direction for decades. Remember back in the day when marketers used mail merge to customize their postcards and letters? Dynamically print a name in the header, and voila! You've got a custom message. Response rates ticked upward, despite the fact that the rest of the letter was identical for everyone.

Along came email, and marketers were able to do the same thing—only far more effectively. Email service providers and early versions of marketing automation platforms (MAPs) gave us the power to segment and dynamically create emails for various types of customers. As a result, engagement and conversion metrics shot up yet again. As these platforms became more sophisticated, we gained the further ability to customize additional elements in the email—such as the header image, the call to action, or designated snippets of copy—based on a known demographic or firmographic data. And, again, we saw a significant improvement in conversions.

Next came the ability to present more targeted information on our landing pages and websites. This was a significant advance and promised to deliver even higher engagement and response rates. And for those companies that were able to do it well, it delivered. As marketing systems advanced and began collecting data on individual behavior and devices using cookies, a very accurate picture of an individual's online persona suddenly became available. This was the sea change marketing had been waiting for all these years. Collecting, managing, and using this data changed the conversation from mere customization to true personalization. Cookies provided hard evidence of past behavior that could be used to craft messages at the individual level and deliver those messages at the right time of day, via the right channels. Personalization at scale, the holy grail of marketers everywhere, was finally within our reach.

By matching a cookie with an online identity, it is possible to pull data on industry, company, title, and any number of firmographic or demographic data elements that can power the ability to speak directly to an individual, even if you don't know exactly who they are. With the right tech stack, an organization can deliver a personalized experience on the first visit to their website by stringing together various technologies and building an accurate profile of the person. Here's how it works.

Let's imagine a website visitor is the VP of finance for a large bank on the East Coast of the United States. Based on these data elements, captured and stitched together from data augmentation services, as well as a recorded history of the visitor's online behavior, a very sophisticated marketing organization can dynamically present a homepage personalized for that individual. The hero image could be a picture of a large bank or storefront, maybe a graphic or cartoon of Wall Street, or anything a creative mind can imagine. All of the case studies displayed could be from customers in the financial sector. The copy blocks could use VP-level messaging relating to ROI or other value propositions relevant to a senior leader. The online bot could be programmed to mention how the company helps senior leaders in financial services solve complex issues. All of this is on the target's first visit. The site appears to have been developed specifically for this VP, all in real time. The person doesn't need to know that, when their managers visit the site, the messaging and imagery change to reflect a different perspective or that, when someone visits from the manufacturing sector, the site experience would be completely different.

We can take this one step further by connecting our MAP to our customer relationship management (CRM), and now we can present an online experience that takes into account existing prospects or customer data collected through our own systems. A customer may have purchased one piece of an integrated solution in the past, and through data mining and analysis, we know that customers that have bought that first module typically buy the second module six to eight months later. Tying the CRM to the website means you can start presenting messaging related to the second purchase as they continue to visit your site, ultimately guiding them to the sale.

Eventually, this customer will need to renew their contract. Depending on your unique purchasing cycle, you could begin presenting value messaging around renewals six months prior to that contract expiration when they visit your website. All of this and more is possible when your systems are synced. It's pretty incredible when you think about what a talented, creative, and determined marketing team can execute when it comes to curating a personalized experience. This is not some future vision only seen in the movies; the technology to make it a reality exists today.

But here's the catch. Because technology has become so powerful, there is a temptation to think that the technology itself is the answer to successful digital transformation. You would be forgiven for thinking that's true. But as I've tried to outline so far, technology is only one of three pillars necessary for true transformation. It's a powerful one, and probably the easiest to implement, but it is a mistake to think that technology alone can deliver the value that you seek.

Don't be fooled into thinking that technology can compensate for or eliminate gaps in your team's capabilities or your processes and workflows. Technology can be a wonderful vehicle to help you scale volume and improve performance, but it is neither a panacea nor a cure-all for an underperforming marketing organization. It may be easy to write a check and install a new platform, but the value from your investment will only be realized through a thoughtful, disciplined approach to the implementation itself.

Today's technological capabilities allow marketers to execute four strategic activities that can deliver scalable revenue:

- Optimize the use of data
- Enforce a well-defined security and privacy policy
- Deliver personalization and customization in real time
- Visualize performance

Easy, right? Let's tackle it.

OPTIMIZE THE USE OF DATA

First on the list is data management. For marketers, this typically takes place within your MAP. It is the repository of contact information, firmographic and demographic information, and behavioral data for all of your customers and prospects. Comprehensive management of this data is what powers much of marketing's arsenal of activities. Email platforms, if not integrated as part of the MAP, tap into this data as part of any outbound activity. Nurture campaigns use this data to make sure the right prospects are getting the right messaging, as do targeted invitations to webinars or events. Having an efficient data management system is a critical table stake of any modern marketing tech stack. Without it, sophisticated or scalable campaign activities are impossible.

Having a data management strategy is one thing, but implementing it is quite another. We've all heard the phrase "garbage in, garbage out," and truer words were never spoken. The importance of data quality and hygiene cannot be underestimated. In fact, the first piece of advice I would give to anyone starting a business would be to always, always, *always* be attentive to prospect and customer data hygiene. Many problems arise from poor data management. From the mundane, like bloat stemming from duplicate records to more crippling issues, like multiple sources overwriting existing fields, a lot can go wrong that can prevent your organization from extracting the true value of one of the company's most valuable assets. Avoiding these issues from the beginning can be achieved by making the building and implementation of a data-quality strategy a top priority.

Elements of this data strategy include a strategic approach for data collection through each and every channel, a hierarchy of tiebreakers that identifies winners and losers when there is a conflict between data sources, and a regular cadence for data clean-up across the entire organization. We can examine each of these in turn.

The value of a data strategy lies in the fact that there is a data strategy. What I mean by that is there are any number of ways to collect, store, manage, and delete data. What's important is that you are doing all of those things with clear intention, to achieve a stated goal. Want to increase the size of your prospect database as your top priority? Make it easier for prospects to complete forms. Want to minimize the number of false data records as your number one goal? Establish a deduping process to eliminate duplicate records? Whatever the ultimate goal, document a process to achieve it, and periodically assess its effectiveness. I've never been at a company where the data was pristine, even after we made it a priority.

The place to start is by examining how and what you're collecting today. What are the current sources of prospect and customer data? If your environment is anything like those I've experienced, I can almost guarantee that there are multiple sources of incoming data. Some are obvious; others might be more obscure. Form completes are obvious ingest points for any database, but what about when a current customer gets promoted and the customer care organization updates their title? Does your data strategy accommodate that? Chances are you may not even be aware of all of the input and edit points of your prospect and customer database and almost certainly don't control them either.

In addition to auditing where the data is coming from, it's equally important to understand what types of data are being collected. If any of it is personally identifiable information, this will have a big impact on privacy or security concerns.

An important but secondary question is this: Is the company taking action on the data being collected? If the answer is no, then why are you collecting it? Data storage and management is not free; it has both direct and opportunity costs, and no one should be collecting data just for the sake of it. This is not to say that it is unwise to collect data if you plan to use it in the future, but unless you have direct plans to do so, it usually makes sense to refrain from collecting it in the first place.

Once you've got a clear picture of who is collecting data and why, the next step is to ensure the usage of this data is aligned with a comprehensive strategy. This isn't an exercise for marketing alone. Working with other parts of the business is essential in order to make this not only as efficient as possible but also yield the desired outcomes. Because databases overlap and interact on a daily basis, and at times, the lines of ownership of the data blurs, it behooves a sophisticated organization to manage data as a strategic asset.

In my own experience, the business intelligence team took ownership of customer data, but only from a presentation perspective. They owned the pane of glass only and were not responsible for maintaining the quality or quantity of the data. This presented all kinds of issues and dispersed data ownership across almost every line of business in the company. The primary outcome of that policy was everyone prioritized their own data and were constantly overwriting values in someone else's data set. That's a recipe for disaster.

This is why any adjustments that need to be made to how data is being collected should be socialized with the other parts of the business, and any collection processes that are not aligned and approved by the group should be eliminated. You don't want to make the problem worse by continuing bad habits.

Once the strategy has been identified and agreed on, the next step is understanding how it will be maintained. There are many facets to this, but the most important one is to implement a hierarchy of truth. Data is collected from multiple sources across the entire organization, and no one group should have the sole accountability of owning all of the data. That's because there will inevitably come a time when two different data sources are trying to populate the same field. The job of the hierarchy of truth is to define a decision tree for how tiebreakers will be handled.

For example, let's assume that one of the data fields you care about is industry. Industry field values can be sourced from multiple systems using various methods. Industry is a common data point associated with cookies, and your website analytics platform can pull that data from the system and populate that field in the MAP. That field can also be populated by the individual when they complete a form to register for a webinar. If there is a divergence between those two values, which is correct? Does a self-identified industry trump a cookie data append? Maybe, maybe not. If the industry field on the landing page is freeform, maybe they invented a new industry by mistake. Or even if it's a drop down, do you trust that they were 100% honest in their submission?

Another consideration, simple on the surface but complex in the application, is when a company uses multiple data sources that provide the same field values. For example, you may use a third-party data-append service that maps firmographic and demographic data fields to device cookies while another third-party service appends objects in your CRM database. These two sources may not share the same definitions, indeed it may be different from the one used even by your own organization, and reconciling these discrepancies through the use of clear definition and decision trees is required if hygiene is to be maintained and quality is to be preserved. As you can see, there are lots of things to think about when it comes to managing your data.

Because most marketing organizations have access to multiple data sources, to say nothing of different parts of the business, they are in a good position to lead the charge when it comes to solidifying a data management policy. Certainly, they have a lot to gain or lose by getting this right, and taking the reins can help you shape the conversation so that your needs are considered. However, that doesn't mean marketing gets to make every decision or that all ties go to marketing. Working closely with sales, sales ops, customer success, finance, legal, and even product will pay dividends down the road in increased productivity for the entire organization.

Given the many questions and considerations, the most important thing you can do is to be deliberate in your strategy. It's ok to tackle this in phases, with a regular cadence of reflection to evaluate whether the current policy is working or needs to be adjusted. Start with marketing data sources, and then work your way out into the business at large. This isn't a decision to be made once and then never revisited. Data management is a living, breathing organism that requires care and feeding at regular intervals.

Data hygiene is not a destination, but a journey. Make sure you know where you're going and how you plan to get there. Once you have a documented and disciplined approach, the next important consideration is privacy and compliance.

DEFINE AND IMPLEMENT A SECURITY AND PRIVACY POLICY

To paraphrase a quote popular in the scientific community about the speed of light, "Data hygiene isn't just a good idea. It's the law." Data privacy as a legislative topic is complex, international in scale, constantly evolving, and fraught with peril for those organizations that choose to ignore it. Fines are significant and enforceable, and while today's technology allows users to do incredible things, some of them are illegal, depending on the location. Consequently, there needs to be documented proof that the system is complying with all local rules and regulations concerning personally identifiable information. Without it, you're playing with fire.

What does this look like in practice? In short, it means having a documented, published policy that outlines the company's practices for treating customer and personal information. Rules and regulations concerning this type of information vary at the international and even regional levels and demand attention wherever your company operates. It is essential that you work with your legal team to understand your leadership's comfort level with using data to personalize marketing messages. Some may be willing to incur more risk, while others are more conservative in their approach, particularly those that count governments as their customers. While marketing often errs on the side of being aggressive, it will ultimately be the legal team's responsibility to address any customer or consumer challenges. As such, it is critical that both teams are part of this process and understand the rules of the game. Trust me when I say that no marketer wants to be out in front of their company's security and privacy policies when individuals or governments start to litigate.

There are some guidelines to consider. First, working with governments typically requires more stringent privacy and data management policies, especially those that work with customers that require security clearances. Companies that sell internationally typically require more comprehensive policies, because the legislation varies widely among countries and regions around the world. Security and legal teams often don't know the full capabilities of marketing platforms and need to be educated on what is possible, let alone permitted. There is a balance to be struck between revenue and other business objectives and privacy and security concerns, which may be somewhat at odds with each other. Most technology vendors are aware of and embrace the fact that companies must comply with a multitude of legislation, rules, and requirements, and their platforms can be customized to adhere to individual company policies. These same vendors typically write disclaimers into their contracts that place responsibility for obeying applicable laws squarely on the shoulders of their customers. The take-home lesson is that you shouldn't expect vendors to take on the liability of getting this wrong.

I am not in a position to provide specific guidance on what is the correct level of concern for privacy and security. Where your organization ultimately lands will depend on lots of competing priorities, but you need to know that marketing can and should take a leadership role in developing these policies. In my experience, most legal and security teams are conservative by nature and will usually err on the side of caution. However, an overly restrictive policy may blunt much of the effectiveness of a modern marketing revenue engine. You will not win every battle, and honestly, you probably shouldn't. But you need to be engaged in the process and be a powerful advocate for the technology because it really can deliver significant improvements in conversions, ROI, and top-line revenue growth.

DELIVER PERSONALIZATION AND CUSTOMIZATION IN REAL TIME

The core of digital transformation's value proposition is to deliver a unique message to a specific individual. To access all relevant data sources and characteristics to conduct personalized one-on-one conversations to increase engagement and value, for both the consumer and vendor, is the end game. As I've discussed, it's the technology that makes this possible.

This drive to personalization, however, consists of far more than a technical implementation. Beyond the technology is another critically important aspect that must be integrated into any marketing organization's efforts to digitally transform consumer expectations.

In the past, there used to be a tangible divide between what people expected as personal consumers and what they had to tolerate as employees. In my own career, I can remember commiserating with my team early and often about how getting anything done at work was always so freaking hard. "Nothing is easy" defines our workplace experience.

Over the last decade, things began to change as the lines between an individual's work and personal life have become increasingly blurred. With e-commerce, one-click shopping, home delivery, and mobile apps, our at-home experience is becoming a seamless integration between technology and the back-end processes that address our wants and needs. Need to check the weather? Ask Alexa. Need a ride to the airport? Order up a Lyft. It's safe to say that engaging with technology has never been simpler or more powerful.

Why is this important? Because companies in the B2C space that improved the customer experience through convenience and personalization, long before their B2B brethren, showed the power of this approach and reaped the financial benefits. As B2B marketers, we should aspire to do the same for our buyers.

We can and should build journeys for corporate buyers that deliver a level of friction-free satisfaction similar to those that we all enjoy in our private lives. For those companies that are doing it now, they will enjoy a significant competitive advantage over those that aren't. The foundation of this experience is personalization.

Speaking directly to an individual, at scale, is hard. Yet evidence suggests that you can drive an increase in conversion rates somewhere in the neighborhood of 10%–15%[2] if you do it well. There are lots of points in the buyers' journey that lend itself to personalization—some might say every point—and multiple systems and technologies that can provide it. To simplify this

---

2   Matt Ariker, Jason Heller, Alejandro Diaz, and Jesko Perrey, "How Marketers Can Personalize at Scale," *Harvard Business Review* (November 23, 2015).

discussion, I'll focus on two systems that can provide a significant level of personalization with not a lot of investment, either in time or money. These two systems are your MAP and your content management system (CMS).

Like nearly everything else, it makes sense to put a strategy in place before committing to a process or piece of technology. To begin, you need to identify what level of personalization is to be achieved. Embracing a crawl–walk–run approach can be useful in this situation. Choosing one or two elements to personalize to start can simplify a lot of the complexity while still allowing for greater sophistication downstream.

Within the MAP, a great place to start the journey is with your nurture streams. For example, your MAP can easily reveal which assets prospects engage with during their visits and enable you to make informed assumptions about their stage in the buyer's journey. Building a nurture strategy targeting individuals at various stages of the journey with email is a relatively simple exercise. Once these nurture streams are activated and automated, it's a hands-free way to continue serving up tailored content and messaging that accelerates their progression through the funnel.

That is only one suggestion of using your MAP to personalize a journey. It's a simple one that nearly every marketing organization, regardless of its sophistication, can employ. As you build up your capabilities and confidence, you can start implementing other best practices, such as connecting the MAP to the CRM. This connection enables all kinds of personalization opportunities, from providing sellers real-time notifications when customers are exploring certain parts of the website to automated email or chatbot engagement based on past customer purchases and contract renewal dates. Once you have the foundational technology in place, the possibilities are limitless, bound only by your imagination.

The second platform that lends itself well to personalization is your website CMS. Dynamically displaying web content based on behavioral, firmographic, or demographic data, as opposed to generic content, can deliver significant conversion rate improvements. Updating hero images, copy blocks, case studies, and other content based on known data points turns a one-size-fits-no-one website into a personalized experience. A more sophisticated (and usually expensive) CMS usually has quite a bit of native functionality to personalize content on the website. But even if you have a more modest CMS system, there are technologies available that can overlay your existing pages with personalized content without updating the underlying code. These systems can also facilitate multivariate A/B testing and often have native connections with other third-party data sources that can personalize further.

When these two systems are working in tandem, it can become really powerful. Add to that the fact that you can integrate data segments within the CRM and the MAP with third-party ad serving to retarget visitors and prospects with ads hyper-personalized based on their behavior.

Personalizing the experience on your website and then leveraging that data into a more targeted nurture campaign positions your company as a trusted advisor that can help the buyer frame and eventually solve their challenges. It's a curated experience that engages them on a deeper level, removing friction and building a deeper relationship. Who wouldn't want that?

Well, the answer to that question is actually "Maybe a lot of people." At this point, I feel compelled to comment a bit about what I call "the creepy factor." Personalization techniques can be employed today that cross the line between engaging and ewwww. The first time someone visits your website is typically not the time to reveal everything you know about them. If they feel like they're being stalked or that you know way more than you should at this stage of the relationship, the probability of a negative experience is very real. In layperson's terms, you don't want to freak people out.

That's why it's important to work with your senior leadership teams to outline exactly what the company is comfortable with when it comes to personalization. Inevitably, someone will be skeeved out by the experience and will make some noise about invasion of privacy and Big Brother keeping tabs on us all. At that point, you'll be grateful that the legal team and CEO were complicit in the development of the strategy and policy. So be sure that any implementation of personalization is managed strategically and with good intent. If done right, you will reap the benefits of a more compelling and meaningful customer journey.

VISUALIZE PERFORMANCE

There is one final practice area that needs your attention if you want to fully harness the power of technology in your digital transformation journey. You need to build a system that can tell you exactly the performance of every single asset on the market, in real time, to power data-driven decision-making that improves ROI. The challenge is that there are multiple systems collecting data, each of which has its own approach to data visualization that may or may not meet your needs.

Web metrics captured in an analytics platform like Google Analytics or Adobe Analytics are crucial data points for understanding what is working in the market. Generally speaking, platforms like these have robust reporting and visualization capabilities that provide real-time assessments of tactical performance. Measuring things like site traffic, unique visitors, page views, time on site, conversions, and more can give you an accurate representation of individual tactics and how your outbound activities are performing. Digital marketing and campaign or program leaders should be armed with this data and use it constantly to optimize channel performance.

Where these systems tend to break down is connecting this online behavior with converted leads and opportunities in the pipeline. The MAP does a good job of tracking lead data, and if it is synced with the CRM, connecting those leads to opportunities is straightforward. However, it's been my experience that while the data is there for sophisticated reporting, the visualization capabilities of these platforms leave a lot to be desired.

Many marketing leaders spin their wheels and throw tons of money at trying to achieve a consolidated view from first visit through deal closure, but that's a fool's errand. The biggest reason to not attempt to deliver one dashboard to rule them all is that it is not a very useful perspective. Dashboards should be constructed to enable data-driven decision-making—nothing more. One dashboard that tells the comprehensive story from first visit through closed-won is not something that can be used in that fashion.

Different roles need different levels of reporting, and some existing tools have robust metrics and visualization capabilities. It doesn't make a lot of sense to try to recreate a sophisticated visualization of online performance in the CRM when one already exists in one of your other platforms. For example, enterprise versions of web analytics platforms have excellent reporting and visualization capabilities when it comes to visitor behavior. It would take an enormous amount of effort to port all of that data into the CRM, and even then, the reporting capabilities on custom objects will necessarily be less advanced than on those out-of-the-box fields.

The same is true for pipeline reporting. Exporting the lead, contact, account, or opportunity data for presentation in a web analytics platform is equally futile. Trying to force the square peg of leads and opportunities into the round hole of visits and time on site is quite simply a waste of time and energy. Leverage the power of the individual platforms and push that data into the hands of the people that need it.

After building the proper dashboards and visualizations, your next job is to empower people to use what you've built. This means making sure the right roles have access to the right information, training them on its use, and setting clear expectations about use. A simple way to standardize operations is to only accept reports using the approved systems. Digital and campaign teams should focus on website analytics. Campaign and business development representative teams should focus on lead creation and opportunity conversion. Managers and directors should focus on balancing investment and channel optimization. Senior leaders should focus on strategic objectives and marketing ROI. One or two dashboards at every level are sufficient to enable data-driven decisions—the end goal of any digital transformation.

These reports can and should use existing visualization capabilities of the native platforms whenever possible. At the tactical level, this makes the most sense, because they are designed with that in mind. But for upper-middle or senior-level marketers who need a more strategic view, it's time to invest in a visualization platform that pulls data from various systems.

The goal is to ingest data from one or multiple systems and leverage the power of the visualization tools to tell a story with the data. Conversion rates, pipeline coverage, weighted pipeline, and sales velocity are just a few of the metrics that marketers need to embrace if they strive to optimize marketing ROI. The accuracy of those reports comes directly as a result of the data coming from that single source of truth, which has the halo effect of building credibility with the sales team. But in order to tell the full story, a visualization suite can be just what the doctor ordered.

LEVERAGING THE TECHNOLOGY

I'll remind you one more time to always build and manage your tech stack with the overall mission of the team in mind. And don't forget that technology will not fix people or process gaps. While it's of vital importance to the overall puzzle, it is not by any means sufficient on its own. More than anything, it is a wonderful catalyst for automating operations for scaling throughput. And when you have the basic principles covered, small incremental improvements can yield big results.

BUILD A ROADMAP

The best place to begin is with a map showing where you want to go. Building a wish list of what you want to accomplish as an organization, without applying any specific technology, can save you a lot of brain damage downstream. Want to build a machine that surrounds 500 companies for truly integrated account-based marketing? That requires certain technology investments. Alternatively, if you're looking to find 100,000 prospects that share similar characteristics (i.e., look-alikes) with your ideal customer profile, that will require something else entirely. Determining what you want to accomplish is job one; determining the specific capabilities required to achieve your goals follows. You don't need to invest too much time and energy into building this map; things will evolve over time, but a well-defined vision is an important first step.

MANAGE EXPECTATIONS

Next, it is important to manage expectations—yours, the team's, and the entire organization's. A common mistake is to buy a bunch of technology all at once and cram it together right away. This typically requires a large initial investment, typically accompanied by a lot of pressure to deliver ROI very quickly. This is a dangerous trap, and the savvy leader would be wise to avoid it.

By embracing a crawl–walk–run approach to your technology investments, you can avoid much of the confusion of buying and using new technology—and, more importantly, avoid the disappointment of unmet expectations. Starting small and achieving incremental success lays the foundation for further investment. Delivering a 5% increase in lead volume or a 5% decrease in cost per acquisition will likely impress those that control the purse strings, who will then likely want to accelerate these gains. Then you've got them right where you want them.

I've lived through two major digital transformations in my career; both were exciting, challenging, a lot of fun, and extraordinarily difficult. In the first, the demand generation team worked very closely with a dedicated MarTech team. Even though everyone was very collaborative and got along well together, there was tension between the teams. As part of the demand generation team, I was eager to get the machine up and running so we could start to deliver more revenue. That enthusiasm was shared by the campaign and programs teams. We couldn't wait to get our hands on the new tools and start creating the magic.

The MarTech team was eager to get started as well, but on a daily basis, they demonstrated they were more enlightened in their approach to technology: what it could do and—more importantly—what it couldn't. They pumped the brakes on requests to purchase new and exciting tools and accelerated the implementation of the ones we already had because they knew what I didn't: that a poorly implemented tech platform in the hands of people that haven't been properly trained is not a recipe for success.

They brought a strategic approach to the process that delivered true value much more quickly than if we had just jumped in with both feet. This approach challenged us to think about what capabilities we would actually use. What decisions would we make if we had access to certain types of information? How would our campaigns and programs evolve as a result of these new capabilities? Do we even have the resources we need to use and support the desired toolset? When we were able to provide meaningful answers to these questions and more, the MarTech team set about identifying, sourcing, and implementing the right technology.

The result was that, over the course of about 24 months, the company went from having absolutely no idea what kind of value marketing was delivering to a real-time dashboard showing performance by region, channel, industry, and several other dimensions. Their approach was the right one, and mine definitely was not.

I'm also not too humble to admit that I brought this new enlightened perspective to my next job and adopted many of the same principles. Over the years, the team I joined had evolved in a haphazard way, purchasing lots of technology in the search for the holy grail, and yet they still couldn't report on marketing's effectiveness with any credibility whatsoever. We set about to replicate what we had just built at my previous job, and by using this strategic crawl–walk–run approach, we were able to create that real-time dashboard in about nine months.

While that may seem like a long time, it's important to remember how everything is interconnected. Quite literally, it can be a case of Whac-A-Mole, where you fix one thing only to discover three others that need your attention. Not to mention the fact that previous decisions often have to be undone before new processes or systems can take effect. Finally, not every change can be applied to data retroactively, meaning the good stuff is only from this point forward. In my specific example, we reconciled all our technology investments, sunsetting three platforms and bringing in three new ones that were better suited for what we were trying to accomplish.

Most importantly, we were focused on the change-management aspect of our digital transformation. This meant ensuring the people that were tasked with using the technology, old or new, had the training they needed to be successful. We provided training programs, timelines, and expectations, and ultimately pushed the expertise out to the edges of the team so that the technology we had purchased was being leveraged for the forces of good by those whose own roles depended on its proper use. When we were comfortable, were using the technology we already owned, and had a good idea of where we wanted to go, only then did we start looking for additional tech to add to the stack. Consequently, the team was definitely walking, maybe even jogging, within the span of 18 months.

All of that is well and good, but what are the foundational elements of a tech stack that can provide transparent revenue at scale? It starts with a strong, adaptable CMS to optimize and personalize your website. You need a MAP to track and manage your prospect data as individuals engage with your outbound activities. While marketing may not own this platform, a powerful CRM system is required to manage leads, opportunities, and customers. Next is a powerful analytics platform—one that can identify and track visitors to your website. Finally, you need a visualization tool that can consume data from multiple sources and offers robust reporting and visualization capabilities that will power data-driven decision-making. These are the five key elements that form the core of a modern demand generation engine.

Let's take a closer look at each of these technologies and why they are important.

CONTENT MANAGEMENT SYSTEM (CMS)

There are a lot of different CMS platforms on the market, and the one you choose depends largely on where you are in your company's evolution. Sophisticated platforms with a plethora of functionality may be just what the doctor ordered for a well-established company with hundreds of thousands of customers and prospects. Yet the same platform may be overkill for a six-year-old startup that is looking to establish itself in the market. Whatever your circumstances, it's important that you build for today's requirements with an eye toward the future.

But not too far in the future. It's easy to over-buy when it comes to technology, and the CMS is no exception. If you want to do some basic personalization using the CMS, a more modest platform that's significantly less expensive is a good choice. Most technology contracts these days are built on three-year terms, so unless you are planning to expand your capabilities at the speed of light, three years of modest capabilities will not negatively impact your personalization activities during that time frame.

The key here is to determine your expectations for the CMS. Will it need to dynamically serve individualized messages at scale on every page? Or will you be content, for the time being at least, conducting more modest A/B testing and limited customization by adding a layer over specific web pages? In other words, does the personalization and customization happen at the CMS level, or are you going to leverage other technology to overlay your site?

If the former, investing in a more robust CMS with advanced digital asset management capabilities makes a lot of sense. If you plan to create layers on top of your site by using third-party applications like Optimizely, a basic CMS may be good enough. And yet another thing to consider as you build out your personalization roadmap: some MAPs provide this layering capability as an add-on, obviating the need for advanced CMS capabilities and offering the ability to leverage a tool that you're already paying for.

MARKETING AUTOMATION PLATFORM (MAP)

The MAP is a system that enables you to track and manage prospect and lead data, build lead scoring models to qualify leads based on activity, manage campaign taxonomies and naming hierarchies, launch and manage landing pages and forms, and automate other activities that are key to turning your ecosystem of prospects into paying customers.

Again, if there is an exception to the rule about hiring for expertise first, this is the place to do it. A MAP jedi will make the whole marketing engine more efficient. They can eliminate bottlenecks and obstacles, develop tests and best practices for lead collection and management, provide insight to extended teams on the performance of tactics and programs, and more. There's simply no end to the value a strong, certified individual can provide with a modern MAP.

The three most important activities that this guru should focus on are segmentation and list management, urchin tracking modules (UTMs), and opt-out compliance.

Segmentation and list management are important for two critical reasons. First, advanced segmentation allows for more targeted messaging and engagement strategies, which—if done appropriately—lead to increases in conversion rates and overall pipeline efficiency. Getting the right content in front of the right person at the right time, using the right channels, is critical to campaign performance, and list building expertise can help ensure you are able to take advantage of such opportunities. Of equal importance is list hygiene. Prospects that change jobs, data that goes stale, errors in the data, and the use of fake names are just a few examples of why active data management is important. Lists that are well maintained are accurate and current and are necessary to the success of any demand generation engine.

The second important activity of the MAP specialist is to develop and implement the UTM strategy. The goal of UTMs is to truly understand which specific tactics create leads, opportunities, and eventually wins, which means that tracking every single asset with a unique UTM is critical. As prospects engage with these assets and come to your landing page, the MAP collects the UTM data and tags the individual appropriately. This tag follows the contact as they move through the funnel, which allows for reporting on individual campaign tactics and reveals the eventual ROI of that particular activity. If the UTM strategy is sound, you can roll up all of the individual leads into campaigns, regions, industries, or any other dimension, depending on what's most meaningful to report on. Without the MAP, this simply is not possible.

Finally, and most important to your legal team, the MAP is where you manage opt-out and privacy compliance. Establishing a bulletproof process for deleting information on request, ensuring opt-outs are suppressed from outbound tactics, and being able to prove that customer data has been removed from the system is critical today and will only become more important in the future. With legislation addressing privacy concerns becoming more stringent around the world, a robust privacy and data security policy, managed and documented in the MAP, is the best defense against significant fines or other penalties.

The MAP is a key cog in the machine for building a revenue engine, but if you don't connect it to the next piece, your ability to optimize performance ends at lead creation.

CUSTOMER RELATIONSHIP MANAGEMENT (CRM)

Your CRM platform, which technically is not a piece of marketing technology at all, is just as critical to building a transparent and scalable revenue engine as anything you'll implement on the marketing side. It is where the sales teams manage their opportunities and pipeline and where they spend nearly all of their admin time (or, at least, where they *should* be spending it). It is also typically the system that is used to measure sales performance. Any credibility that marketing hopes to achieve comes solely from being able to link to and use the data that exists in the CRM. Because of that, I'm including it in this list of core technology.

I am not suggesting that marketing take ownership of this platform. It is a complex system, and sales ops needs to be responsible for its operation and management. What I will focus on are the four key processes that integrate with the CRM and have a direct and significant impact on marketing's ability to do their job:

- Connecting the MAP to the CRM
- Synchronizing the data between the two systems
- Managing time stamps, stage progression, and conversion rates

• Pulling data directly from the CRM for pipeline reporting

Connection

To enable transparency, the MAP needs to connect to the CRM. Without knowing the conversion rates from leads to wins, as well as deal size, there's no way to be certain what value marketing added to the pipeline. You may say, "We delivered 100 leads," and that should equate to $1 million in revenue. My response, and probably sales's as well, would be "How do you figure?" A hundred leads, even if they're qualified, don't necessarily equate to anything. A hundred leads that never became opportunities are just noise. And if the MAP is not connected to the CRM, it takes a whole lot of manual labor and mental gymnastics to figure out which leads converted to opportunities. That's why connecting the MAP to the CRM needs to happen before you focus on anything else. Without that connection, there is no credibility.

Synchronization

Connecting the CRM to the MAP is one thing; the next job is to sync them—regularly. Typically, this synchronization doesn't occur in real time—not unless you've got a super sophisticated, automated engagement system that requires lightning fast response times. Weekly is far too much time. A good (and generally effective) guideline is to sync the MAP and the CRM every day. This powers the ability for performance management and SLA reporting and prevents errors from becoming serious issues due to a lag time. MAPs are built to connect to CRMs, so this shouldn't be technically difficult, but only the inexperienced aren't periodically ensuring the sync is as intended and that any reporting is pulling from the latest data.

Progression

When the MAP and CRM are connected and syncing, the next step is to start actively monitoring and optimizing marketing's contribution to the pipeline. This entails using timestamps and calculating conversion rates. If you are using UTMs (and you'd better be!), you can measure conversion rates based on channel, region, asset type, etc., to get a very sophisticated and powerful model of what tactics are delivering real value at every stage of the funnel. Value not just in lead creation but also in opportunity creation and, eventually, wins. Even if you aren't operating at that level of sophistication, by observing how leads and opportunities are progressing through the various stages, you'll gain insight into possible improvements, where to double down, and where to take your foot off the gas.

Reports

The last important piece that needs to be considered for the CRM is your reporting. As with statistics, reports that are generated in your CRM can mean almost anything to anybody, depending on the filters used to generate it. Marketing may want to see how many leads converted to opportunities and can apply filters and generate reports that provide that insight.

However, sales may have a different view on what is meant by *lead* or *opportunity*—or *source* or *timing* or lots of other things— and when the reports don't agree, everyone loses credibility. That's why it's important to start with common definitions. If there is alignment on what each stage means and what needs to happen to progress to the subsequent one, any discrepancies can be attributed to filtering, which is a much easier problem to solve.

I've been involved in too many meetings with the CEO where marketing says one thing and sales says another. Both are true based on the data in the system, but they don't agree with each other. Nobody wins in that situation. The answer is to ensure that the reports that are shared outside the marketing organization are developed jointly with sales. This may mean compromising on the view, but it is a lot better than presenting contradictory or confusing information.

Some reports that I have used in the past that have been well received and that you may want to consider are weighted pipeline coverage and marketing sourced revenue. We filtered these by region, by company size, by deal size, and by a few other dimensions, but at the core, these reports answered the important questions: "Do we have enough revenue to cover our targets for the year?" and "Is marketing going to meet their obligation to the business?"

Now, the answer to those questions was not always yes, but because the data came from the CRM and we were committed to transparency, we established a higher level of trust with our sales counterparts. It was only at that point that we achieved true alignment between the marketing and sales team on measuring performance and establishing mutual accountability. Hooray!

ANALYTICS

What are the analytics platforms that compose the core engine? The bad news is that there isn't a single platform that can provide all the answers. There are three dimensions that must be accounted for when creating a report, and no single system that I've encountered is capable of accommodating all three.

The first of these is the audience. This data—and the insight derived from it—varies based on who is using it. The digital team will be looking at things like site traffic, pages visited, engagement metrics, and other dimensions that enable them to optimize their tactics. The CMO is interested only academically at that level and is more concerned with things like marketing ROI and contribution to revenue. Who is using the data determines in large part which platform is best suited to delivering the reports.

The second dimension is cadence. How often does the data need to be refreshed? Again, using the website as an example, a daily view of visitors will be important to identify seasonality or performance spikes like a press release or product announcement, while closed revenue may be reported on a monthly basis. The cadence for any given report will depend on how quickly action needs to be (or, frankly, should be) taken based on the results.

Finally, the third dimension is the message. What is actually being conveyed by the report, and what decisions will be made based on the results? Is it tactical, such as cost per click or form completion rate? Or is it more strategic—things like weighted pipeline coverage or sales cycle velocity? It's probably easiest to think about the CMO's report to the board for this one. It's unlikely they will care too much about extracting $.01 per click from a display ad, but they will be very interested in knowing pipeline velocity or revenue coverage.

The altitude, cadence, and message will dictate the analytics platform and required reporting, and not the other way around. A savvy marketer understands this and leverages the appropriate platform for the right scenarios.

TRAPS AND PITFALLS

There are two pitfalls to be aware of as you execute your reporting strategy. I've mentioned these before, but they bear repeating. Don't spend too much time looking at the same data through a slightly different lens. And don't try to measure everything under the sun.

There is an almost irresistible temptation to continue tinkering with reports and slicing and dicing the data in a thousand different ways. There may be a little value in this exercise, but most of the satisfaction comes merely from scratching that itch to look at things from a slightly different perspective. Resist this temptation. Identify and socialize a small number of key reports and stick with them. Focus your energy on improving performance, as opposed to spending time manipulating the reports themselves. I am as guilty as anybody when it comes to this, but I've learned over time that generating numerous different perspectives generally doesn't add much value or lead to better insights.

The other temptation is to report on literally every single data point stored within the system. Once again, there is a lot of satisfaction to be derived from looking at performance across every kind of data object—but there is usually very little value to be found. Here's a good guideline: If you're not going to take action based on the report, you don't need it. For example, if you're not going to target customers from companies with annual revenues between $100 million and $150 million any differently than companies with annual revenues between $200 million and $250 million, then don't measure it. It might be interesting to look at, but it's wasted effort, plain and simple.

The simplest advice I can give someone who wants to leverage analytics for continual improvement is this: Before you build or review a single report, ask yourself, *What question are you trying to answer?* Are you going to behave any differently based on the results? Who needs to use the report? How often does it need to be refreshed? And what is the message that will be delivered based on the report? If you can answer all of these, and you still want to see the data, build the report.

With all of this in mind, here are the key platforms that I recommend you employ in order to build that high-performance engine.

Web analytics

Free versions of web analytics software are everywhere, with the 800-pound gorilla being Google Analytics. These can be powerful tools, they are generally easy to use, and the price is right—three really good reasons to use these to get started. In fact, most are robust enough that they are capable of supporting an organization through its first $50–$75 million of revenue. However, once you start spending seven figures on your marketing programs, it's time to graduate to an enterprise-level platform. The additional functionality, customization capabilities, and sophistication are critical if you hope to drive omnichannel performance improvements at scale.

Visualization

Once you've identified the core reports you will use to gauge and improve performance, there may be an opportunity to combine some of these more tactical reports to tell a more nuanced and comprehensive story. I'm speaking mostly about pipeline reports at this point, for a couple of reasons.

If you have any experience with CRMs, it will come as no surprise that the reporting and visualization capabilities of those platforms is mostly *meh*. From usability to the colors of the graphs, it's one disappointment after another. Consequently, I would suggest investing in a visualization platform. These systems can pull data from multiple sources and create compelling views that allow for easy comprehension. They are also easy to manipulate and customize and, therefore, result in intelligent, data-driven decision-making.

You would be well served to engage your business intelligence team, if you have one, to help connect some of the dots. Getting professional help in making sure the right objects are being mapped appropriately is critical. Errors committed during this process result in bad decisions, so it is important to get it right.

At one company, the database team was relatively inexperienced and was still figuring out how to use their tools. They also had no experience supporting a marketing workflow. The result was a series of mistakes that took us months to hunt down and rectify, with no accurate reporting in the interim. It was a bit of a mess, and like touching a hot stove for the first time, it was an experience that I will not forget.

The good news is that, when these maps are built correctly, you'll have a powerful and informed view of how all of your tactics are performing. This is crucial, because it enables your team to optimize for all the right things—and ultimately deliver the real value of digital transformation.

Integrating data from the CRM and the finance and accounting platform offers insight into marketing's ROI, weighted pipeline coverage, and marketing's contribution. It can be filtered by geography, industry, company size, and any other meaningful object in the database. Want individual performance on your campaign managers, sales development reps, and account executives? Here is where that happens. All of the insight you'll need to make improvements across the entire marketing ecosystem and revenue funnel is unearthed when you possess this type of reporting capability. It is absolutely worth pursuing if you hope to achieve true transformation.

These are the four key elements that you need to get started with your digital transformation. Employing the crawl–walk–run model means you can get started with sophisticated programs that make a significant impact on performance with relatively small investments in technology. As you gain confidence and increase investment, you can start to expand your tech stack to take advantage of new opportunities and watch your marketing ROI grow correspondingly. For some relevant tools and templates, refer to Appendix C.

The bottom line when it comes to technology is this: technology has incredible power to create a more meaningful and compelling experience for your target audience. It has equal power to alienate and freak out your customers and prospects—and maybe get you fined. The way to strike the right balance is by establishing a data management policy, engaging legal and security to ensure your compliance with all legal and company rules and regulations, improving your customer's journey by speaking to them as an individual, and creating a small but comprehensive set of dashboards that power your engine of continuous improvement.

Chapter 4

LEADING THE CHARGE

Realizing the full potential of marketing's digital transformation means building an intricate machine with many moving parts. It's a complex operation requiring strategic vision and attention to detail. This means trusting your team, and yourself, and having the will to persevere in the face of steady headwinds. It means having a vision of where you're going and the determination to keep the team focused on the future. And it means prioritizing the important things, while still being flexible enough to make adjustments along the way.

With your digital transformation roadmap now in place, it's important to take a minute to think strategically about the leader's role in the journey. There are six important activities that, if done with regularity and attention, can greatly enhance your team's chances of successfully implementing this transformation.

The first is to create a vision. Your job isn't to tell everyone what to do but to offer an exciting and compelling view of the end state that will ultimately pay dividends to your team and to the larger organization.

The second is to establish clear priorities. You must stay focused on only those tasks and processes that can actually move the needle. This takes effort, concentration, and unwavering commitment.

Next is to provide protection. Your team needs your support in providing consistent and fierce defense from all of the inevitable requests and other noise that threatens to distract them from their goals.

The fourth is to remember to celebrate incremental successes. The best way to build and sustain momentum—as well as team enthusiasm—is to recognize that things are changing for the better. Showcase and celebrate those milestones in a visible and positive way.

Next, it's extremely important that you are visible, accessible, and present during this process. Being there for the team is about more than answering questions or securing resources. It's about being what your team needs, when they need it, at all times.

Finally, trust your team. It sounds simple, but it can sometimes be hard when tackling something as challenging as a digital transformation. However, even if it requires more work in the short term or learning a few things the hard way, a team that is built on trust will nearly always outperform those that aren't.

CREATE AND COMMUNICATE A VISION

Digital transformation is not a project that lends itself to a numbered list of clear directions. It is complex and evolving, and the more time you invest ensuring everyone knows what success looks like in the grand scheme of things, the more time and effort you will save downstream. The goal is to create a high-performance revenue generation engine built on transparency and accountability and capable of generating predictable revenue at scale. The most efficient way to do that is to establish clarity and enthusiasm around the future state and empower your team to achieve results. While this revelation is not exactly revolutionary, as leaders, the temptation to simply tell people what to do can be strong and extremely difficult to resist. You must resist if you hope to get the most out of your team and deliver the best possible results for your company.

Communications, analyst and media relations, product marketing, and other areas of marketing all play a key role in the overall success, but for our purposes, we will assume they are all operating efficiently and are, therefore, beyond the scope of this example. For now, we are prioritizing top-line revenue growth as our primary objective.

Your first job is to make sure everyone knows what success looks like. The status quo is an insidious creature, creating a gravity well that saps the will to innovate. Change is usually difficult, seemingly impossible at times, and without a clear vision of how things will be better in the long run, it can be challenging to get people moving in the right direction.

As leaders, we create that vision by quantifying marketing's contribution to revenue as a percentage of overall growth. New logo revenue comes from many sources; channel partners, sales, and prospecting are probably the biggest aside from marketing. Whether or not your company keeps score on where this revenue comes from, the important part is that, added all together, it covers the growth target for the year. Marketing's role in this process is to identify and commit to a number that they will source and work to deliver against that target. To do this requires a system that can measure and track revenue associated with marketing's activities.

This may take a bit of time, particularly if the required infrastructure is not yet in place, but that's ok. While we're doing that, we can start to benchmark and optimize program and channel performance and conversion rates, which will help lower the cost per acquisition of leads, increase pipeline revenue coverage, and ultimately increase the return on marketing investment. It seems like a lot, and it is, but focusing on our key areas of people, process, and technology will help us get where we want to go.

Beyond the numbers, a vision of the future that is recognizable and attainable can get people excited and aligned—especially if you help them understand what's in it for them. Focusing on how the team's everyday lives should become better by exchanging inefficient, mundane, and repetitive tasks for more strategic, value-added work is a great place to start. Professional satisfaction typically increases when workers feel their work has value, and automating uninteresting tasks can have a measurable impact on the satisfaction levels of the team.

Also, being personally involved in a digital transformation initiative that results in significant improvements in marketing performance creates opportunities for professional growth and career advancement. Whether their contributions lead to an internal promotion or whether they choose to take their talents somewhere else, it's hard to deny the value associated with creating a high-performance revenue engine and the transferability of those skills. In short, there's a lot in it for them, at a personal level, to be part of a successful digital transformation.

Ensuring that your team recognizes all of these benefits is your responsibility and will be the rocket fuel that powers the journey.

PRIORITIZE THE IMPORTANT PARTS

Once there is a vision to rally behind, the next job is to prioritize the key initiatives that will deliver the most value. There is always more work than time, and it is very easy to get distracted by the tactical imperatives of the day, jumping from one hot spot to the next. Establishing clear priorities (and being ruthless about adhering to them) not only focuses energy where it will have the greatest impact, but it will also provide your team with the freedom they need to succeed.

PROTECT FROM DISTRACTIONS

Perhaps the greatest gift you can give your team is permission to say no. It's impossible to overestimate how liberating and empowering this simple idea can be, and it is a powerful boost to team morale, cohesion, and efficiency.

Steve Jobs once famously said, "People think focus means saying yes to the thing you've got to focus on. But that's not what it means at all. It means saying no to the hundred other good ideas that there are." We've all been asked to accept a new assignment, task, or responsibility without first negotiating what comes off the list. I know I have, both as the giver and the receiver. In fact, I do it more often than I should. Yet it's one of the biggest risks to successful digital transformation. There are countless good ideas, new processes, and technologies that could genuinely improve the engine. But not all of them will contribute equally, and not all of them will work well together. That's why it's so important to establish the goals first and say no to anything that doesn't directly support them.

Along with reinforcing the priorities with your team, you need to be doing the same thing with your peer group at the organizational level. Some call this "air cover"; for others, it is "running interference." Regardless of what you call it, it is extremely important that other leaders around the company understand what marketing's priorities are and how these will benefit the entire organization. Not everyone will recognize or accept your team's attempts to say no. Where competing priorities and ideas come together is where you are needed most, and you can avoid a lot of tension and friction by being proactive in your communications with your peer group.

Finally, the permission to say no only comes from the top, and it's extremely important that you live by the same rules. If you do not embody this culture of saying no, your team will not feel empowered to do it either. As I mentioned, I've found myself taking on additional responsibility for the team that was outside of our established priorities on more than one occasion, so I recognize how difficult this can be. It is important to recognize that not all bullets can be dodged, but your default position should be to remain focused on the established goals. Other projects are the exception, not the rule. Only personally modeling this behavior will give your team confidence to do the same.

CELEBRATE VICTORIES ALONG THE WAY

Celebrating small victories consistently and publicly is one of the best methods of generating and maintaining momentum. The team will need (and appreciate) an infusion of excitement and will build on them to accomplish bigger and better things. They need not be expensive, overwhelming, or even completely serious.

One of my previous teams recognized a "friend of sales" at the go-to-market all-hands meeting every month. The sales team would nominate individuals from outside the core group that really helped move the ball forward for sales during the month. There was no monetary incentive or even physical reward, but the recognition in front of the whole GTM team was very motivating for the winner and even the other members of the extended team. To see that sales was taking the time to highlight contributions of other teams was a big deal for everyone in the organization. It was also a bit of enlightened self-interest in that it garnered a lot of political capital for the team, which they used to ask for favors. People were happy to help knowing they were being recognized as a key contributor to the success of the company. Take this lesson to heart and remember that what's important is that you're recognizing the time and effort being spent on your team's transformation and that you see things changing for the better.

Digital transformation is a long and challenging journey. It can sometimes feel insurmountable when viewed in its entirety. Breaking it up into smaller, less intimidating chunks and celebrating their completion can help people marshal the necessary strength and motivation to keep fighting until the end.

BE VISIBLE, ACCESSIBLE, AND PRESENT

A successful leader is one who creates teams that are greater than the sum of their parts. And the successful leaders I've worked with were not carbon copies of each other. They each had their own perspectives, strategies, backgrounds, and styles of communication. They were unique, and yet they were able to create an esprit de corps that delivered impressive results.

But there was a common thread among them all: They each went out of their way to be visible, accessible, and—most important—present. No business school secrets, no high-powered executive training, just a dedicated approach to being there for their team.

Being visible isn't just accepting awards when things are going great. As a matter of fact, it is quite the opposite. Any sports fan will tell you that, when teams win, good coaches praise the players. When the teams lose, these same coaches take responsibility for not preparing their players. In short, wins belong to the players, and losses belong to the coach. The same is true when leading a digital transformation.

It means being an enthusiastic and consistent advocate for the team. It means being the point person when negotiating necessary changes with other parts of the organization, particularly when they may be unpopular. It means celebrating individual successes by calling attention to them publicly. Supporting your team by ensuring they have what they need to do the job, as well as by providing the air cover and prioritization to help them stay focused, will not only pay organizational dividends but will help motivate the team on an individual basis because they know you have their back.

Next, it's important to truly be accessible. This goes beyond simply having an open-door policy. It means being open-minded and understanding that good ideas come from everywhere. Accessible leaders are not married to their ideas or their way of doing things. They are willing to be challenged—expect it, even—and encourage the team to explore new and better ways of doing things. They don't pretend to know everything and are confident enough to ask for help or clarification.

You must also be present. Time together as a team or on an individual basis is focused, collaborative, and positive. At its most basic, it means turning off notifications and closing the computer. On a deeper level, it is being what each team member needs. Any effective leader will tell you that not everyone responds to coaching the same way. Some need to be challenged; others need encouragement. A great leader takes the time to know what each of their team members needs to be successful—and is adaptable enough to provide it.

TRUST THE TEAM TO DO THE RIGHT THING

Last, and perhaps most important, leaders need to trust their teams. If you've done a good job of defining success, identifying key objectives, and tending to the emotional well-being of your team members, then your trust will not be misplaced. While the team may not do things exactly as you would, if it accomplishes the goal, who cares? A good leader knows good ideas come from everywhere, and giving your team the space and authority to do things their way will build confidence and capability quicker than almost anything else. When they feel they are trusted, they will be willing to challenge the status quo and take the kinds of calculated risks needed for true digital transformation to take place.

I once had the good fortune to work for someone who really understood what it meant to leverage the strength of her team. Each of her direct reports was an expert in their own right, with decades of deep experience, and we didn't need anyone to tell us what to do. So, she didn't even try. She asked questions out of genuine curiosity, to challenge us to constantly improve, and as a means of coordinating our efforts. She could have exercised her institutional authority and exerted control for its own sake, but she resisted the temptation—and we were all the better for it, as was the company. Embracing these leadership habits fostered a loyalty that turned the team into a motivated, collaborative force that fundamentally changed marketing's value to the company. Her leadership made a huge impact on both morale and the ability to work as a cohesive unit.

Leading a team through a digital transformation is a challenge like no other, and it's inevitable that your team will feel overwhelmed at times; you will too. Embracing these leadership principles can boost your team's morale and create an environment for them to be successful by securing for them the plan, the resources, and the confidence they will need to achieve these lofty ambitions.

ACHIEVING THE OPTIMAL BALANCE

Needless to say, simultaneously managing the people, processes, and technology required to digitally transform (all while being the leader your team needs) is a significant undertaking—and one that often fails to meet expectations. The reason for this usually isn't a lack of perseverance or the absence of technical know-how. Rather, it comes from an imbalanced investment of time, energy, and money. This asymmetry of investment, both too much and too little, is responsible for the majority of failed experiments, so it makes sense to briefly explore what this looks like in real life so you can recognize the signs and make course corrections as needed.

PEOPLE

Underinvesting in the team itself comes in two flavors. First and the more obvious of the two is "Do you have enough?" The knee-jerk answer is always "No, we need more people, but resources are limited, so we have to make do with what we have." This tension, while uncomfortable, can be useful when going through a digital transformation. It forces you to focus on those things that will make the biggest impact. It means you prioritize what can give you the much needed cover when other requests are made to the team.

Also, while there are some cases where additional people are absolutely required, in most cases, expanding the team also contributes to inefficiency at the same scale as before. In other words, more people don't usually improve efficiency. It may increase throughput but will simultaneously generate the same amount of proportional waste as before. That's great if your organization can afford it, but it's not the ideal situation. Consequently, prioritization can be an effective weight-loss strategy to combat organizational bloat.

The other type of underinvestment is not having enough of those critical characteristics and cultural similarities. This issue is harder to address. Finding individuals with that crucial mix of curiosity and determination can be difficult. If you're new to a team, you may have inherited a group of individuals that were hired for completely different purposes by someone with different priorities. If you're a tenured member of a team, the digital transformation initiative itself may be new. In either case, it's possible that the hand you've been dealt is not the hand you need to win—and it's time to up your investment in the team.

If your team is composed of individuals that inherently lack natural curiosity and determination, they are more likely to succumb to the inertia of the current environment. Some team members may be frustrated by the ambiguity and fluidity of the transition, or they may have a hard time envisioning the end state. These team members will likely drag their feet, acting as an albatross around the neck of the rest of the team that delays—or even halts—progress. The transition will be hard enough with everyone rowing in the same direction, and if someone isn't onboard, you'll end up going in circles. If that's the case, you aren't doing your team any favors by forcing them to come along on this journey. Respectfully helping these individuals find something else to do—either internally if there is a good fit or outside the organization if there isn't—is essential. Not everyone is suited to be part of these initiatives. There is no shame in it, but you'll need to find those who are in it to win it if you want a shot at success.

For those team members with the right character and attitude but who lack the skills needed to perform in this new environment, training is the way to go. One indication that training is needed is an increase in the number or type of questions being asked. If a team member used to ask more strategic questions but is suddenly asking more tactical "how do I"–type questions, this may indicate they're not familiar with the tools or processes. Similarly, where they may have been very proactive before, you may now find that they're waiting for more detailed guidance. Both of these may indicate they need some additional training or support.

To rectify this situation means an investment in coursework, conferences, certifications, or other types of training. Yes, it's time and money allocated to something other than generating revenue, but until your team members are able to contribute regularly and in a meaningful way to your digital transformation initiative, your efficiency and momentum will suffer. I've personally found that investing in training and education for team members repays itself several times over through improved performance, better morale, greater loyalty and enthusiasm, a higher degree of job satisfaction, and an infectious optimism. That rising tide lifts all boats. It is also a visible and powerful signal to the rest of the team that you're willing to invest in their personal success, which triggers others to seek the same type of self-improvement. It can be a virtuous circle once it gets rolling, and the actual out-of-pocket costs are typically pretty small when compared with the collective gains.

Now that we've discussed the ramifications of underinvestment in people, let's move on to the consequences of *over*investment. While it's impossible to find someone with too much curiosity or determination, it is absolutely possible to overinvest in the size of the team. Hiring too many people is as wasteful and inefficient as not having enough. One of the core strengths of digital transformation is that the machine, once it is built and operating at scale, does not require an army of people to increase throughput.

An example of how machines can help you scale throughput without adding headcount comes from attending the Adobe Summit a few years back. At one of the keynote sessions, Adobe unveiled AI technology that was capable of building a media plan. They actually constructed one in real time during the presentation, taking about five minutes, while they discussed how their AI was taking all of these variables into account to build the plan. The crowd was duly impressed. What used to take a team of experts several weeks to develop was delivered by a machine in just under five minutes.

Now, this is not a story about how machines are coming for all of our jobs. But it does show that AI and machine learning will be replacing some of the repetitive parts of our jobs in the near term, freeing up people and resources to perform higher-value work. The demand generation engine operates under the same principles. When the technology automates nurture campaigns, advertising activations, audience segmentation, and other activities once handled by people, scaling throughput no longer requires additional headcount—or, at least, not to the same degree as before.

A final point about balanced investment in your people pertains to providing input and guidance to the extended teams outside of marketing as to the right size of the downstream teams that will be supported by marketing. I've lived through times where the sales development rep (SDR) team was much, much larger than the programs team designed to feed it. The same was true for channel and partner marketing. These teams kept growing with no commensurate investment in the demand team or programs to support them. The result was a lot of hand wringing, as well as mismanaged and unmet expectations, as to what the demand generation engine was capable of delivering. In one specific example, the SDR team had over 20 members that needed care and feeding from a demand team roughly half that size. To make matters worse, with our existing acquisition costs, the marketing budget was roughly one-tenth the size it needed to be to fully support that many SDRs. Needless to say, there was a lot of tension between the two teams, and not much of it was healthy. It's impossible to control investment across other lines of business, but you need to be proactive in highlighting asymmetry when you see it and, whenever possible, quantifying the impact.

PROCESS

The critical error of underinvesting in the process is very common. It is a mistake to shortchange the process when it comes to documentation, execution, and optimization, especially the documentation part. How things get done from day to day can evolve in all sorts of ways—some logical, and some not—and often the only documentation is someone named Dave (and the only reason he knows is because he's been here the longest). Not knowing why things are done the way they are done is bad enough. But not knowing *how* they're done is even worse. As the old axiom goes, "If you don't know what's broken, how are you going to fix it?" Process optimization is impossible without first knowing what needs to be fixed, and there are no alternatives to doing the detailed work of documenting the processes.

There are several recognizable signals that suggest there is work yet to do in documenting processes. They commonly surface during onboarding when someone new asks questions about the how and the why. If you are unable to provide a process document in some way, shape, or form for your important processes, you've got some work to do. When you've got a repeatable and disciplined process that can be easily explained to a new employee, that's when you know you've done enough. It doesn't have to be perfect—in fact, it almost certainly won't be—but getting it written down is the first step to bringing the consistency required for improvement. Then and only then should you start the optimization process.

What does this optimization process look like? It depends heavily on the individual process being optimized, but there are a few tried and true methods you can employ that will help, regardless of what is being targeted for improvement.

First and most important, implement a change-management process. Yes, this is a process for improving your processes, but it is the best way to introduce disciplined, repeatable steps that greatly enhance the likelihood of success. I've worked in organizations that religiously adhered to a change-management strategy, and I've worked in organizations where it was the Wild West. I think you can guess which had more success.

Next, don't develop and launch a process change in a vacuum. Socialize it. Ask other parts of the business if they have one, and if so, what do they like about it, and what would they change? Work closely with sales ops to jointly define a process-improvement process so there is alignment on goals and shared visibility into the end results.

Important note: No process change should ever be revealed on the go-live date. No one likes surprises when it comes to new processes—and I mean no one. Make sure anyone who will (or even might) be affected has the opportunity to review the proposed changes and provide feedback. You might be surprised at how often recommendations surface that enhance the process. What matters is that you embrace a change-management process, and give people a heads-up before implementing it.

Next, have a sense of urgency, and convey it widely. Process change, by its very nature, is difficult and will take as long as you let it. Set dates and milestones, and insist that you and your team members be governed by them. Be realistic and disciplined. Ensure the team has the resources they need, and hold them accountable. Without a ticking clock, it is very easy to lose momentum.

Finally, be agile in your approach. It is impossible to predict with 100% certainty exactly what a process change will deliver, and being agile in your change-management strategy and approach can embrace this ambiguity. Processes should never be etched in stone. Talented teams constantly challenge the status quo and are looking for ways to tweak things for greater efficiency. Embracing flexibility means incremental improvement can be a constant, never-ending journey to optimization.

With all of that in mind, it is important to also recognize that you can invest too much in process. Although much less common, organizations have been known to get lost in the details in trying to establish their workflows. Complexity for its own sake is a form of asymmetric investment, creating inefficiency and confusion for no discernable benefit. The lead passing process is a good example where overengineering the workflow can have significant negative impacts on the efficiency of the pipeline. SDRs are living, breathing, thinking individuals that can assess lead viability or assignment requirements much faster and more efficiently than writing every eventuality into the code. Being too rigid in the application of process rules can sap morale from the team, dampen creativity, and reduce agility. None of those, obviously, are conducive to a high-performance revenue generation engine.

Getting the process right by finding the right balance between rigidity and agility will take some time. Embrace the fact that these processes need not be poured into concrete; in fact, they absolutely shouldn't be. Think of them more like Legos—easy to assemble, rigid enough to hold their shape, but very easy to disconnect, redesign, and build anew. As long as you're attentive to those processes that are critical to the success of your engine and are open to change to improve performance, you should be ok.

TECHNOLOGY

We come at last to technology. I've spoken ad nauseum on the dangers of overinvestment in technology. Buying too much, too fast, without proper change management and training leads to unfulfilled expectations and disappointment. Inevitably, leaders find that technology alone cannot compensate for shortcomings in their teams or their processes. So, what are the warning signs that you may be underinvesting? If you have a lot of manual, repetitive processes that hamper your ability to scale, that's one dead giveaway. I'm reminded of a situation at one of the companies where I worked that struggled with reporting. When I arrived on the scene, it was impossible to quantify marketing's contribution to the revenue pipeline, we didn't know our conversion rates from first visit to deal closure, and we didn't even know how much it cost to create a lead, an opportunity, or a sale. It was an area of great discomfort and exposure for our leadership team and one that needed to be addressed.

After some initial work building taxonomies and adding urchin tracking modules (UTMs) to our marketing tactics, we were able to measure channel performance. With that came some rudimentary pipeline analysis, done using Excel. I had a team member that spent the first week of every month aggregating a bunch of data from multiple systems and creating the mother of all pivot tables. He had to do a lot of manual filtering to ensure quality, and even then, the overall results were dependent on data from other business systems that had no governance or oversight. It was so squirrely that we felt it necessary to provide a full page of caveats for just the first chart! Regardless of the overall accuracy or validity of the reports, it literally took my guy five working days—slightly less than 25% of a full-time equivalent—to compile the report.

Fast-forward a couple of months, and we had purchased and implemented a UTM management tool, integrated the marketing automation platform with the customer relationship management system, and layered a visualization suite over the top. We were now spending just 15 minutes per month to accomplish a task that previously took a week, with a much higher credibility factor. It wasn't that we didn't want to measure and report on our performance or even that we didn't know how. We just didn't have the right tools at our disposal to do it right. With a deliberate investment strategy that followed a three-year roadmap, we brought in the right technology that allowed us to answer specific questions about marketing's contribution to revenue and provide those answers to the board. And that's just one example; I have dozens of others, all of which tell a similar story.

Suffice it to say that if expectations for marketing's performance are increasing, you need to make sure you're investing in the right technology that will allow you to meet those goals. In the example I just gave, it meant benchmarking conversion rates, cost per acquisition, pipeline coverage, and channel performance, as well as executing personalization at scale for all website visitors. It's just not possible to do these things with a tech stack consisting of only Excel and Mailchimp—as awesome as these tools are. Sooner or later, you need to graduate to professional tools. Just make sure you're doing it with a plan, a purpose, and a schedule.

Asymmetric investment is the root cause for most digital transformation failures. Finding the right number of the right type of people is critical to the eventual success of any transformation. Neglecting process documentation hinders improvement as surely as too much rigidity will stifle creativity. Not having the right tools and technology in place limits the ability to scale revenue, while relying too heavily on technology to solve personnel and process issues is equally restrictive, not to mention wasteful. A balanced and disciplined approach that matches investment across people, processes, and technology is the best way to deliver on the promise. Think Goldilocks. You don't want to do too much or too little in any one specific area. You want everything to be just right.

BRINGING IT ALL HOME

Digital transformation is an extremely satisfying journey, but it is also incredibly challenging. In fact, making the commitment to undertake the journey at all is the most important first step. And when, eventually, after many trials and tribulations, you achieve that coveted end state of consistent, predictable revenue at scale, two things will happen: First, you'll feel an immense sense of satisfaction. The hard work is what makes it worthwhile. And second, you'll immediately recognize other opportunities for improvement. (What—you thought there was a finish line?)

If I were to pick a metaphor to describe what digital transformation is, I would suggest that it is like a high-wire act between two buildings. On one side is subjectivity and marketing's inability to quantify its contribution to the business. On the other is a simple equation that balances expense and revenue. And the only way to get from point A to point B is by traversing a wire suspended between the two buildings. A disciplined, careful, and—most important—*balanced* approach is the only way to get to the other side.

It's ok to admit that it's hard. In fact, if it's not hard, you're probably doing it wrong. And because of the difficulty, progress will be measured in months or quarters, as opposed to days or weeks.

Keep in mind that every high-wire act has a safety net below. It is possible—likely, in fact—that, at times, you'll lose your balance and fall. But you can always climb back up on the wire and continue the journey. With vigilance, determination, discipline, and hope, you'll make it to the other side.

Remember also that digital transformation is not binary. It isn't either a roaring success or a dismal failure. It is possible that you'll make a lot of progress, build and nurture a wonderful team, improve a lot of processes, and add some new cool, powerful technology but *still* not have the world's most sophisticated revenue engine. And that's ok. If you take the agile approach and build with continuous improvement in mind, you will constantly be creating value, which is what any great marketing team does.

I hope I've been able to provide some useful guidance for those undertaking their own digital transformation. As I said at the outset, now is marketing's time. The potential for us to change the narrative from one of subjective optimism to predictable accountability is enormous. With it, we can fundamentally redefine what marketing can be to organizations and take our rightful place at the executive table, comfortably standing toe to toe with finance and operations when it comes to quantifying ROI and building the business case for investment. It's a day that is long overdue but that is sweet in coming, and it's something that we should all celebrate.

PEOPLE

To help jump-start your efforts, here are some tools and job posting templates that you can use to build the people part of a revenue generation engine for your unique circumstance. It is doubtful that you will be able to (or even should) plug and play many of these assets without customizing them in some way, but they can provide enough structure for you to implement the crawl phase of your transformation. From there, you can evolve over time to really drive that change.

SAMPLE ORGANIZATIONAL CHART

A simple org chart would look something like this, with five core functions supporting the digital and offline generation of leads and opportunities. They include digital, analytics, programs, field and events, and automation.

Depending on the revenue targets and appetite for expense, the size of the team can flex. One of the biggest advantages provided by the digital transformation is that once you have the foundational elements in place, it becomes much easier to scale revenue production without adding additional headcount. The machine delivers greater efficiencies over time by leveraging disciplined processes and marketing technology.

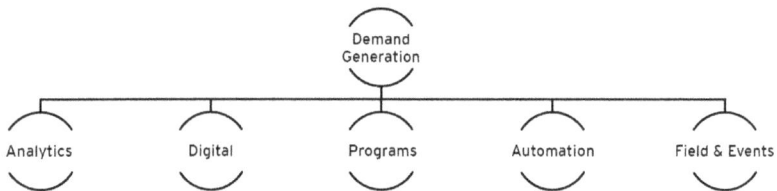

As was mentioned in the text, it's possible for a single individual to perform several of these functions, but these types of revenue generation engines are not well suited for single-person start-up environments. Typical benchmarks suggest that marketing spend as a percentage of total revenue can vary between 3% and 15%. Companies that are more mature (i.e., have the capacity to spend more or have more modest growth targets) populate the low end of that spectrum. Companies that are attempting to grow very quickly live at the high end. This can have a big impact on the size and sophistication of the marketing organization, specifically the demand generation team.

Based on the expense of building a high-performance team with access to the right technology to drive revenue at scale, top-line revenue targets of more than $3–$4 million a year are the starting point. Anything less than that, and you likely won't be able to afford—nor will you need—the machine.

To generate $3–$4 million a year in new revenue would best be served by the org structure outlined above, but could probably survive by combining the digital and automation or analytics and automation function together, at least initially.

JOB DESCRIPTIONS
DIRECTOR - ANALYTICS

Activities

- Analyze and execute data for marketing
- Set up custom reporting, funnel, and analyze web analytics data to drive insightful learnings and testing opportunities to improve conversion rates and revenue
- Communicate complex data analysis into easy-to-understand bullets to explain the story behind the numbers and share actionable recommendations
- Partner with program, digital, and field marketing managers to design promo testing to evaluate incremental return and margin impacts
- Perform ad-hoc data analysis and create custom reports to service the needs of business partners and leadership teams
- Create internal dashboards that automate key metrics and provide insights into performance within all aspects of marketing
- Evaluate audience segmentation, creative, and other marketing-related A/B tests, and provide recommendations related to experiment prioritization
- Develop models that drive metrics toward improved operations and profitability—i.e., demand forecasting

Experience

- Bachelor's degree from 4-year college or university in a relevant subject (math, finance, economics, digital or marketing analytics, or a related field)

- Minimum of 1 year of full-time work experience in a highly analytical capacity
- 2–3 years' experience in advanced web analytics; certification highly preferred
- Can communicate complex data analysis in easy-to-understand bullets
- Experience with digital media management such as AdWords, Facebook ads manager, Criteo, Pinterest, and similar technologies
- Experience with A/B analysis and audience segmentation
- Self-starter with problem-solving skills
- Experience with Microsoft Office Suite, with particularly advanced Excel skills (vlookups and pivot tables, other advanced formulas are a must)
- Experience with visualization platform (i.e., Tableau, Looker) highly preferred

DIRECTOR - DIGITAL

Activities

- Create plans for web, SEO and SEM, email campaigns, social media and display advertising campaigns across various owned, paid, and earned media
- Design, build, and maintain social media presence
- Measure and report performance of all digital marketing campaigns and assess against goals (ROI and KPIs)

- Identify trends and insights and optimize spend and performance based on the insights
- Brainstorm new and creative digital growth strategies
- Plan, execute, and measure experiments and conversion tests
- Collaborate with internal teams to create landing pages and optimize user experience
- Use strong analytical ability to evaluate end-to-end customer experience across multiple channels and customer touch points
- Understand and implement all facets of lead nurturing and marketing automation, including list segmentation, emails, campaign automation, landing pages, and reporting
- Instrument conversion points and optimize user funnels
- Work with extended teams to ensure digital marketing campaigns are fully optimized and that all required lead acquisition components, lead routing, and processes are working effectively
- Collaborate with agencies and other vendor partners
- Evaluate emerging technologies and provide thought leadership and perspective for adoption where appropriate

Experience

- Bachelor's degree in marketing or a related field of study
- Minimum 7 years' B2B digital marketing experience
- Must have a data-driven approach to marketing; experience using data to refine and optimize digital demand generation and funnel conversion

- Exceptional analytical skills
- Experience with the following digital channels:
  - *Google AdWords*
  - *SEO*
  - *Facebook or LinkedIn ads*
  - *Instagram*
  - *Twitter*
  - *Pinterest*
  - *TikTok*
  - *Other emerging platforms*

DIRECTOR – PROGRAMS

Activities

- Build programs and integrated marketing campaigns to guide prospects through the buyer's journey, leveraging digital and offline channels to generate a consistent flow of marketing qualified leads
- Own quarterly and annual growth targets; manage and monitor program budget and cadence to ensure plans are optimized to achieve program effectiveness, driving optimization and future innovation and meeting company goals for pipeline growth
- Perform project management of marketing plan deliverables, timeline, and production, ensuring campaign, messaging, and branding alignment across channels

- Work with digital and field marketing teams to gain approval of plan and budget, and ensure marketing strategies, tactics, and content align with program strategy, positioning, and objectives
- Track marketing program KPIs, and forecast and manage marketing budget
- Identify and coordinate with external marketing resources and vendors on content development, advertising and media, other partnerships, and additional tactics as needed to execute the marketing plan
- Understand where the program's communications needs and strategy fit in with the broader corporate strategy, and leverage opportunities for alignment
- Gather data and analytics to gauge content and marketing effectiveness, and optimize toward high-performance content and distribution channels
- Coordinate customer testing of campaign assets with the digital marketing and brand team, or participate on teams developing customer segmentation for advertising and communications

Experience

- Bachelor's degree in marketing, communications, or a related field; 5–7 years' relevant work experience
- Proven experience creating, managing, and communicating a marketing plan, content calendar, and production grid while meeting deadlines

- Proven experience writing content for various communications channels—newsletters, email, web, etc.
- Knowledge of best-in-class practices for customer engagement and proven experience optimizing customer engagement strategies and tactics to improve results
- Proven experience managing complex projects with cross-functional teams in an ever-changing and fast-paced environment
- Understanding of the techniques and processes needed to create a consistent and common voice across customer communications
- Excellent verbal and written communication skills

DIRECTOR – AUTOMATION

Activities

- Take ownership of the marketing tech stack by leading the administration and management of integrations, lead routing, field mapping, and optimizations of functionalities
- Troubleshoot and QA workflows, data issues, and other key marketing ops functions
- Manage the evaluation and implementation of new marketing tech
- Optimize marketing automation platforms, lead routers, CRMs, and visualization tools to ensure consistent tracking and routing workflows

- Provide strategic guidance on marketing automation campaigns to program, digital, and field marketing teams
- Support the optimization of lead scoring and routing methodology to increase funnel efficiencies and conversion rates
- Provide thorough knowledge of best practices and processes for marketing automation, and actively drive, organize, and participate in key enhancements in all marketing technology suites
- Quickly implement projects involving diverse and complex data relationships
- Manage the lead enrichment strategy for improving the quality of the database (prospect and customer) to enable effective segmentation and profiling
- Ensure required data is captured at all buyer engagement stages and accurate multitouch attribution is reported
- Work with the team to build marketing analytics reporting and develop insights to make recommendations on areas for optimization and improve performance benchmarks
- Provide leadership in defining, mapping, and documenting key marketing processes

Experience

- 6+ years experience in marketing automation
- Experience working with sales teams
- Strong analytical skills and ability to understand complex data sets

- Proficient user of CRM platforms
- Familiarity with automation rules and triggers
- Proficient user of Excel and other data analysis tools
- BA/BS degree preferred

DIRECTOR - FIELD & EVENTS

Activities

- Work with Program and Digital teams to develop regional marketing plans to support local KPIs
- Create compelling, regional-appropriate marketing programs and events that integrate digital and offline tactics that engage core customer segments
- Build relationships with and engage local sales teams, channel partners and alliance partners to co-own and promote the programs
- Manage key metrics such as pipeline, cost per meeting, cost per lead, opportunity conversion, etc., for the local region

Experience

- 5+ years in a field marketing role
- Strong field and channel marketing expertise
- Ability to create regional marketing plans, communicate those plans, and build buy-in with sales teams and channel
- Strong written, oral, interpersonal, and presentation skills

- Strong project management, negotiation, and decision-making skills

- Demonstrated ability to execute multiple events and programs simultaneously

- Ability to build trusting, collaborative relationships with peers, sales teams, distributors, resellers, and customers

- CRM, marketing automation familiarity a plus

- BS/BA degree or equivalent

·

Appendix B

PROCESS

To help jump-start your efforts, here are some samples and resources that you can use to build the process part of a revenue generation engine for your unique circumstance. It is doubtful that you will be able to (or even should) plug and play many of these assets without customizing them in some way, but they can provide enough structure for you to implement the crawl phase of your transformation. From there, you can evolve over time to really drive that change.

SAMPLE CAMPAIGN TAXONOMY

A campaign taxonomy is a structured naming convention that assigns values to different variables. When those variables are used in concert, the taxonomy can uniquely identify every single tactic. It is the bedrock of all future reporting, and therefore, it's impossible to overstate its importance.

A typical campaign taxonomy formalizes the names of the campaigns and programs, all of the marketing channels that will be used to promote content supporting these programs, the different sources, and finally the various mediums that will be used. It also makes sense to add a descriptor for the asset itself, as well as space to accommodate any marketing automation platform objects, as well as the name of the individual requestor. It sounds like a lot, and it can be intimidating for the uninitiated, but once you lay it out logically, it becomes relatively simple to execute. Large, sophisticated organizations that execute multiple campaigns simultaneously will likely choose to invest in an urchin tracking module (UTM) management platform to automate many of these steps, but that is not a necessity early on in the process.

Remember, the entire purpose of this process is to be able to uniquely identify every single tactic so that you can measure performance at the most basic level as well as roll up groups of activities into more strategic views. I think it's probably easier to show an example than try to continue a verbal explanation, so with that in mind, here is a sample structure to create your taxonomy:

Marketing program	Channel	Vendor	Description	Source	Medium	Name	Submitter	Create date	MAP program

- Marketing program: the name of your campaign or program. "3 ways to improve efficiency," for example. It's the organizing element of all of the various tactics to support a revenue target.

- Channel: the marketing channel used for this particular asset. Examples include email, events, content syndication; they can be either digital or offline in nature.

- Vendor: If you're using an agency partner or channel vendor and you want to be able to measure performance against internal channels or other vendors, use this element.

- Description: a plain-English descriptor of the asset, an amalgam of the source and medium, or something else that you'd like to measure against.

- Source: the tactic's source, typically the proper name of the channel, such as LinkedIn, Facebook, or your company's name in the case of email as the channel.

- Medium: the category of the traffic source, e.g., referral, cpl, event.

- Name: the name of the particular asset, the title of the white paper, or the name of the infographic, as examples.

- Submitter: the name of the marketer who owns the tactic. This enables performance reporting by individuals.

- Create date: when the tactic was created.

- MAP program: definition of specific programs within your MAP. This may or may not be the same as your campaign programs.

When you have solidified this taxonomy, you will be able to measure performance at the most granular levels, powering your optimization over time and scaling revenue.

Building a campaign naming hierarchy is essential for accurate reporting. It's important that you build enough variables into your structure to accommodate today's elements but also to plan for the future. Retroactively adding variables can have serious repercussions on reporting accuracy and may be impossible to apply to past activities. Therefore, even if the current plans do not necessitate adding variables for every available channel, reserving a spot in the hierarchy now will save a lot of brain damage when the time comes to activate it.

SAMPLE LEAD SCORING MODEL

Lead scoring is a critical component of any high-performance demand generation engine. Allocating points in the marketing automation platform based on generic behaviors is the most basic form. As an example, earning 15 points for registering for a webinar is a simple process to implement. As your comfort level and sophistication grow, adding additional elements based on intent signals can yield big results. To take the previous example a bit further, awarding 15 points for registering for a thought leadership webinar, a top-of-funnel asset, but awarding 45 points for registering for a product demo webinar, which is a bottom-of-funnel asset, can increase the velocity of lead creation and improve conversion rates.

Lead scoring models are malleable and should be routinely tinkered with to optimize performance. A/B testing the values of certain activities or increasing or decreasing values based on historical propensity to convert ratios can be done on a quarterly basis. It's more about continual improvement than it is about reaching the optimal state, because times, assets, and buying behaviors are constantly in flux.

With that in mind, here is an sample lead scoring table that is enough to get you started on your own optimization journey:

BEHAVIOR		RULES AND LIMITATIONS	NEW POINTS		
TYPE	ACTION		TOFU	MOFU	BOFU
Email | Clicks link in any Marketo email		Once an hour only	5		
Email | Clicks link in any MSI email		Once an hour only	5		
Event | Clear conference	Registered	n/a	100		
Event | Clear conference	Attended	n/a	30		
Event | Clear conference	Engaged	n/a	20		
Event | Regional or roadshow	Registered	n/a	100		
Event | Regional or roadshow	Attended	n/a	30		
Event | Regional or roadshow	Engaged	n/a	20		
Event | Sponsored	Attended	n/a	15		
Event | Sponsored	Visited Booth	n/a	30		
Event | Sponsored	Engaged	n/a	100		
Event | Tradeshow	Attended	n/a	15		
Event | Tradeshow	Visited Booth	n/a	30		
Event | Tradeshow	Engaged	n/a	100		
Event | User group	Registered	n/a	100		
Event | User group	Attended	n/a	100		
Event | Webinar	Registered	n/a	10	20	30
Event | Webinar	Attended	n/a	20	40	70
Event | Webinar	Attended on-demand	n/a	30	60	100
Instant qualify | High priority | Contact	n/a	n/a	100		
Instant qualify | High priority | The rest	n/a	n/a	100		
Instant qualify | Standard priority | Other	n/a	n/a	100		
Instant qualify | Standard priority | AR + product	n/a	Within 7 days	100		
Referral or purchased list engaged	n/a	n/a	20		
Web resource	n/a	n/a	30	60	100
Web | High value page (products section) visits	n/a	Once a day only	15		
Web | Low value page visits	n/a	Once a day only	5		
Web | Multiple visits	n/a	3+ visits to product pages within 7 days. The person can only run through this campaign once every 3 months.	100		

PIPELINE DEFINITIONS

Clarity around definitions of sales cycle stages is one of the most important things you can do to promote collaboration between marketing and sales. Here are some examples of definitions of the various stages that you can use to get the process started. It's not super critical that you use these verbatim. What's more important is that you have a defined set of terms that everyone agrees on and are used consistently across the entire organization.

Stage	Description
Inquiry (INQ)	The total number of raw responses or hand-raisers to an outbound or inbound marketing activity. Relatively little is known about the prospect at this point.
Marketing qualified lead (MQL)	A lead/contact that has been qualified by achieving a score equal to or greater than 100 points in Marketo and is deemed ready for an SDR.
Sales accepted lead (SAL)	An SDR was able to set a discovery meeting for the contact and the Account Executive. A discovery call task is created, which also creates a Pre-Qualification opportunity.
Opportunity	The Account Executive has a successful discovery meeting with the contact and changes the opportunity status to a value greater than Pre-Qualification, then continues to work the opportunity.
Win	The contact's opportunity is marked as closed-won, indicating a sale has been made and the contact is considered a customer.

UTM RESOURCES

A UTM (urchin tracking module—but no one ever refers to them as such) is a simple code that can be attached to any URL to generate web analytics data for marketing campaigns. They are digital tags that can be used to identify unique assets. It is possible to create UTMs for offline assets as well, as long as you create the appropriate tag at the moment of lead ingestion into the marketing automation platform. For example, downloading the attendee list of an offline event from the booth scanner and uploading into the marketing automation platform can be accompanied by the creation of the UTM at that point of ingestion.

It can be confusing, but again, it's impossible to overestimate the importance of getting these correct as they are the individual bricks of your reporting foundation. If you would like additional information on the definitions, purpose, or usage of UTMs, there are a multitude of references online to help. Here are just a few to help get you started:

UTMs resources

- https://pagely.com/blog/utm-parameters
- https://buffer.com/library/utm-guide
- https://www.privy.com/blog/2018/4/hdtsw-utms-and-mnms

Appendix C

TECHNOLOGY

To help jump-start your efforts, here are some tools and guidelines that you can use to build the technology part of a revenue generation engine for your unique circumstance. It is doubtful that you will be able to (or even should) plug and play many of these assets without customizing them in some way, but they can provide enough structure for you to implement the crawl phase of your transformation. From there, you can evolve over time to really drive that change.

DASHBOARDS

The lifeblood of any high-performance engine is real-time performance measurement that powers continual improvement. Dashboards are some of the easiest and most powerful vehicles at our disposal to deliver this insight. While they are not necessarily easy to build, once it is constructed, it becomes quite easy to scale because the KPIs don't change, and therefore, the dashboards remain constant.

But what should you measure? The possibilities are endless, and therein lies the challenge. Once there is a capacity to visualize data, the temptation to create different views is almost overwhelming. Everyone loves a dashboard; the cool presentation of abstract data is always appealing. However, most everyone also wants a slightly different perspective of the same data to answer a slightly different question.

Consequently, dashboard creation takes on a life of its own, and teams often spend more time creating views than they do analyzing what the views they have are saying. This is a patch of quicksand that has trapped more than its fair share of companies. I myself have succumbed to the allure of "if only we could look at it this way." The danger is real.

To combat this predilection to view the same data through multiple lenses, is to identify the two or three views of the data that are needed to make decisions and then stop. Rather than continuing to tinker with the views, invest that energy working to improve the results of those KPIs that you determined were important. It takes discipline—a lot of discipline—to resist this temptation to build dashboard after dashboard, but those organizations that can focus on a smaller number of key metrics will always outperform those that can't.

WEBSITE

For the web, those key metrics to measure and optimize are visits, engagement, and conversions. You can further slice and dice these three metrics by region, company size, persona, product, and just about anything that you can think of is possible in today's analytics suites. Just remember, if you're continually improving in these three critical areas, you're winning in the market.

VISITS

Visits are the number of unique (and sometimes return) visitors to the site. If your growth percentage is higher than the industry growth rate, you're taking share. It's not a direct one-to-one correlation, but it's close enough to use as a proxy.

ENGAGEMENT

Pages visited and time on site are good proxies for engagement that answers the question "Are your visitors finding interesting content to consume?" You need to be a bit careful about pages visited because that could be a function of poor overall design or site logic, but generally speaking, going to more pages is better than not, just like spending more time is better than spending less.

CONVERSIONS

This is where the rubber meets the road for your entire funnel downstream. Are your visitors trading their contact information for valuable information on your site? Increasing your conversion percentage means you're delivering good value. Decreasing means you're not and it's time to rethink your content strategy.

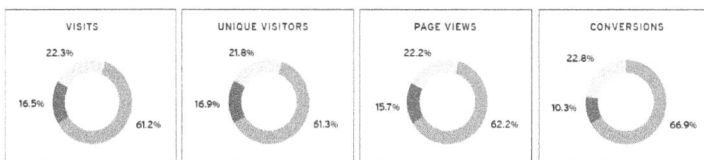

	VISITS	UNIQUE VISITORS	PAGE VIEWS	CONVERSIONS
	22.3%	21.8%	22.2%	22.8%
	16.5% 61.2%	16.9% 61.3%	15.7% 62.2%	10.3% 66.9%

Region

	Visits	Unique Visitors	Page Views	Lead Conversion	Conversion Rate
Segments Page: 1/1 Rows 400 1-3 of 3	262,036 Jan 1 Mar 31	187,672 Jan 1 Mar 31	403,697 Jan 1 Mar 31	12,503 Jan 1	13.3% Jan 1
1) Global Region: Americas	160,365 61.2%	115,071 61.3%	251,024 62.2%	8,363 66.9%	5.2%
Segments Page: 1/1 Rows 5 1-2 of 2	160,365 Jan 1 Mar 31	115,102 Jan 1 Mar 31	251,024 Jan 1 Mar 31	8,363 Jan 1	11.4% Jan 1
2) Global Region: EMEA	58,348 22.3%	40,946 21.8%	89,477 22.2%	2,853 22.8%	4.9%
Segments Page: 1/1 Rows 10 1-8 of 8	58,348 Jan 1 Mar 31	41,097 Jan 1 Mar 31	89,510 Jan 1 Mar 31	2,853 Jan 1	32.9% Jan 1
3) Global Region: APAC	43,323 16.5%	31,745 16.9%	63,196 15.7%	1,287 10.3%	3.0%
Segments Page: 1/1 Rows 5 1-4 of 4	43,323 Jan 1 Mar 31	31,763 Jan 1 Mar 31	63,196 Jan 1 Mar 31	1,287 Jan 1	14.0% Jan 1

Here is what a useful dashboard could look like. In this example, I've shown an additional layer by region. It is important to note that these are super easy to build in any web analytics platform, and if you're not already doing it, you absolutely should be.

Source/Medium	Sessions	% Change	Pageviews	% Change	New Users	% Change	Bounce Rate	% Change	Duration	% Change
Google/organic	7665	938%	10,479	640%	6131	1212%	86%	29%	00:46	-55%
Direct/none	2897	66%	4899	119%	1731	8.5%	84%	1%	1:13	262%
Adroll/display	156	-50%	175	-61%	38	-78%	89%	31%	00:25	-41%
Linkedin/referral	152	-10%	221	-28%	109	-4%	76%	5%	00:36	-70%
Google ppc	79	3850%	100	4900%	60	-	84%	-15%	00:17	-
Bing/organic	70	169%	91	89%	46	142%	81%	11%	00:48	-34%

Of course, these are not the only dimensions available to measure, nor should they be. But they are the first three and should be made available to the entire marketing team, so they are aware of the performance of marketing in general in the market.

PIPELINE

Having a thorough and detailed understanding of the pipeline performance is the single greatest tool in your toolbox for generating revenue at scale. It is the common frame of reference for true peer-to-peer comparison or benchmarking, as well as shining a light on where improvements can make the greatest impact. Because they are linear in nature, there is more leverage for impact the further to the right you progress down the funnel. Consequently, a small increase in conversion percentage from opportunity to closed-won will have a much larger impact than a larger increase further upstream. However, improving the conversion rate at any stage can have dramatic effects on the ability to scale revenue, and therefore, every effort should be made to develop a real-time measurement process for every stage of the funnel from visit through closed-won.

While the conversion rates are extremely important, the output of those rates is what's truly important: revenue. That being said, the most useful dashboard for the CMOs and other senior leaders, including the board, is weighted and unweighted pipeline coverage. Is marketing providing the necessary revenue to achieve the organization's revenue target?

By creating this view, by quarter, it's possible to establish an early warning system that identifies gaps in revenue coverage with enough time to do something about it. This revenue shortfall can come from anywhere—sales, channel, etc.—but marketing is in the unique position of being able to do something concrete to address it. It's an extraordinarily valuable tool, and this is what it looks like:

Unweighted is taking the absolute value of opportunities from the CRM, without regard for the sales stage. It represents the total revenue possible if everything eventually progressed through to closed-won.

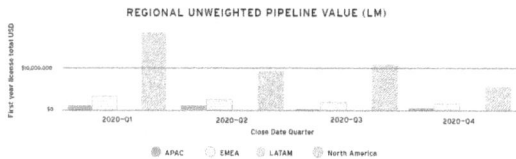

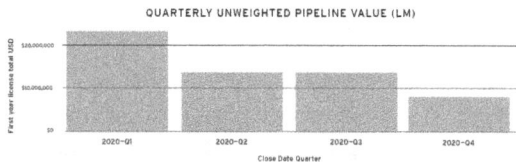

Weighted is multiplying the opportunity size by the expected close percentage. In other words, those deals that are earlier in the sales cycle have a much smaller chance of closing than those further downstream. The percentages used to normalize the data vary by organization, and working closely with your sales ops team, you should be able to determine those close percentages by stage to create what's called a *weighted coverage model*. It takes into account that some deals will fall out of the pipeline. If the sales ops team has formalized this process, the weighted pipeline coverage model is close to an accurate representation of what will actually happen in the future and is a close predictor of actual financial performance. You can see from this example that these numbers are much smaller than unweighted, reflecting the fact that deals will drop out over time.

$15,025,936
Total Weighted Pipeline Value (LM)

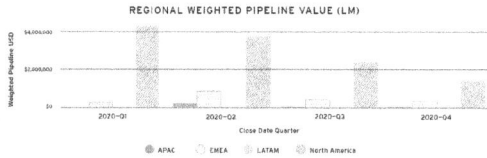

REGIONAL WEIGHTED PIPELINE VALUE (LM)

QUARTERLY WEIGHTED PIPELINE VALUE (LM)

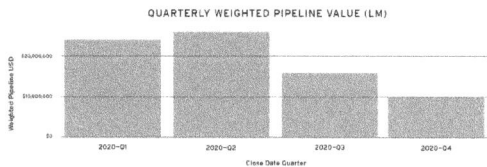

PIPELINE CONVERSION RATE BENCHMARKS

While every situation is unique at the company level and while comparing to peer groups is also nuanced, it can sometimes be useful to use industry benchmarks as comparisons for pipeline performance. With that in mind, here are some generic conversion rates to use to measure yourself against as a baseline.

Benchmark	Conversion rate
Visit to INQ	3%
INQ to MQL	20%
MQL to SAL	20%
SAL to opportunity	60%
Opportunity to win	25%
INQ to win	0.6%

CONVERSION RATE CONSIDERATIONS

Conversion rates calculation is a topic that warrants a book all by itself. There are subtleties to these calculations that uninitiated are unlikely to comprehend and that would take much longer than I have the time to allocate here, but let me just say this: Conversion rate calculation, on the surface at least, seems very simple. It's as easy as dividing the number of individuals in stage 2 by the number of individuals in stage 1. Unfortunately, it is not that at all.

An example may help. Imagine a seven-stage sales funnel, starting at lead and ending with a customer win, with qualified lead being stage 2. One could argue that putting the total of qualified leads in the numerator and the total number of leads in the denominator automatically gives you the conversion rate from lead to qualified lead. And in some instances, you would be correct. On an infinite time scale, with immaculate hygiene, the conversion rate calculation is this simple. Unfortunately, neither of the prerequisites is true.

Consequently, when you start applying a time box to that calculation, say a calendar month, along with unpredictable or undesirable hygiene (funnel fishing, for example), the whole equation starts to fall apart.

To make the math simple, let's assume we generated 100 quali-fied leads and 50 sales accepted leads in January. That would suggest a 50% conversion rate from qualified lead to sales accepted lead. Simple, right? But what about a lead that was created on January 31 and didn't convert within the designated time box? Should that be included? Or, at the other end of the spectrum, should we include sales accepted leads that were created on January 1? You can start to see some of the complexities manifest themselves in this basic example. And that's just the tip of the iceberg. We haven't considered the effects of human errors introduced into the system—a delay in uploading leads from an event, as an example, or a newly minted sales development rep that doesn't know how to make the stage change in Salesforce. There are any number of errors and issues that get introduced, literally every single day, that impact the veracity of your conversion metrics.

Honestly, this is more complicated than anyone who doesn't live and breathe this stuff would believe, so I leave you with this word of caution. Be careful in making broad generalizations when it comes to conversion rates unless and until you are willing to invest the time and energy to truly understand what is happening on the ground. It's definitely worth it to pursue that level of cred-ibility, but it takes commitment and discipline.

REVENUE CALCULATOR

The ultimate reward for all of this hard work comes when you can create a simple spreadsheet to calculate your program expense requirements to generate a specific amount of revenue. When you have the key elements of the equation, the math is extraordinarily simple, and a one-page workbook in Excel can give you the exact dimensions of your marketing program.

To help you quantify these requirements, here are the elements that you'll need:

- *Average deal size:* the amount of revenue, per contract, that best represents the normal engagement
- Pipeline conversion rates: the benchmarked conversion percentages associated with each stage of the sales funnel
- Cost per acquisition of a lead: the amount required to secure a form complete with valid contact information

And that's it. For this example, and to make the math easy, we'll assume an average deal size of $50,000 and will use industry average conversion rates. Here's how it works:

AVERAGE DEAL SIZE

Work with the finance and sales ops team to identify the average deal size for the organization.

Average deal size	$50,000

REVENUE TARGET

Identify the revenue target for marketing sourced revenue. For this example, let's say $1,000,000.00.

REQUIRED WINS

Dividing the total revenue target by the average deal size gives the total number of wins required to achieve the goal.

Total number of wins	20
Marketing sources wins (35% of total)	7

PIPELINE CONVERSION RATES

Pipeline conversion rates are industry benchmarks for B2B companies. Insert your own benchmarked conversion rates to customize your funnel.

Pipeline calculations	Annual
Required inquiries	1166
Organic inquiries	583
Target paid inquiries	583

REQUIRED INQUIRIES

Using industry benchmarks for our pipeline conversion rates reveals how many inquiries are required to generate target revenue.

ORGANIC VERSUS PAID INQUIRIES

The good news is that not all inquiries need come from paid activities. A significant percentage often come from organic traffic to your site. It's a mistake to think these are totally free, however, because investments in brand, SEO or SEM, and word-of-mouth tactics can make a significant impact on the volume of organic traffic. For this exercise, let's assume that 50% comes from organic.

COST PER INQUIRY

Now you have the total number of paid inquiries needed to achieve the revenue target. These can vary widely, depending on industry, offering, etc., and there is usually a big difference between digital and offline. For this exercise, we will use a blended cost per inquiry of $250.

Required INQs (paid)	Cost per INQ (blended)	Marketing budget required
583	$250	$145,833

EXPENSE:REVENUE

The example yields an expense:revenue ratio of roughly 15%, which is mostly in line with industry standards.

ADDING SOPHISTICATION

Once you have the baseline performance metrics in place, it is possible to start building more sophisticated models for improved accuracy. Want to build regional versions using local conversion rates? No problem. Weighted averages of multiple types of deals? Easy. Using channel-specific cost per acquisition values to really refine the engine's performance? Simple. The model supports as much customization as you care to add, with each addition removing a little bit more of the subjectivity that marketing has historically been associated with.

ABOUT THE AUTHOR

E D is a global business-to-business marketing executive with over 20 years of experience helping public, private, and private equity–backed organizations create value through revenue acceleration and organizational optimization. Combining his experience in technology and process improvement with visionary strategy, he has transformed marketing teams to transcend antiquated practices and expectations.

With graduate degrees in engineering and business, Ed brings a data-driven methodology that removes subjectivity from marketing to deliver quantitative proof of marketing's contribution to organizational value. He has helped establish marketing as a competitive differentiator in companies ranging from $30M to over $1B in annual recurring revenue.

Originally from Boulder, Ed enjoys his family, running and cycling, rescuing big dogs, and Charles Dickens.